THOMAS BOUCH

The Builder of the
TAY BRIDGE

THOMAS BOUCH

The Builder of the
TAY BRIDGE

JOHN RAPLEY

TEMPUS

To Graeme, John, Martin and Karen

First published 2007

Tempus Publishing Limited
The Mill, Brimscombe Port,
Stroud, Gloucestershire, GL5 2QG
www.tempus-publishing.com

© John Rapley, 2007

The right of John Rapley to be identified as the Author
of this work has been asserted in accordance with the
Copyrights, Designs and Patents Act 1988.

British Library Cataloguing in Publication Data.
A catalogue record for this book is available from the British Library.

ISBN 978 07524 3695 1

Typesetting and origination by Tempus Publishing Limited
Printed in Great Britain

CONTENTS

ACKNOWLEDGEMENTS

In addition to those named in the Foreword, I would like to thank the following who have all contributed to the information in this book. Since it has been in preparation over a number of years, I apologise sincerely to any whose names have been inadvertently omitted.

Jake Almond, Metallurgist, Estom; Gordon Biddle, Levens, Kendal; Ms K. Bennett, Darlington Library; Andrew Bethune, Edinburgh Central Library; Cumbrian Archives, Carlisle; Ms Sally Deas, Fife Regional Library, Cupar; Alan Earnshaw, Appleby in Westmorland; Jeff Hurst, Loanhead, Midlothian; John Jamieson, Dumfermline Library; David Kett, Dundee Wellgate Library; Ms Margaret King, Angus District Library; John Marshall, Bewdley; Tom Martin, Motherwell Bridge Co.; Iain MacLeod, Glasgow; Charles McKean, Dundee University; Newcastle Central Library; Ms J.M. Parker, Cleveland County Library; David Patterson, Edinburgh Arts Centre; Scottish National Archives, Edinburgh; Ms Marion Richardson, Midlothian District Library; Norman Turnbull, Denholm, Hawick; Stephen White, Carlisle Library.

PICTURE CREDITS

FOREWORD

The 28 December 2004 marked the 125th anniversary of the destruction of the first Tay Bridge during a violent storm. To many this distant date will have little significance, but the folk-memory of the people of Dundee is long, and the story of the fall of the bridge still attracts lively debate. In 1929 there were many still alive with personal recollections of that night, probably the most dramatic event in their lives and the history of the city. By the centenary in 1979 the response was more muted, though two full-length books published earlier had helped to keep memories alive. Nor was it overlooked by the Scottish press. But to a wider public the engineer of the world's longest bridge (over tidal waters to be precise), Sir Thomas Bouch, is little remembered for all his other works, and the story of his life and what he achieved over forty years deserves putting on record.

Whenever the name of Sir Thomas Bouch crops up it is invariably followed by 'the engineer of the ill-fated Tay Bridge', and in consequence he has been dismissed as just an incompetent minor Victorian engineer. Minor engineers do not build the world's longest bridge and receive a knighthood from a grateful Sovereign, nor would they venture to build the world's longest spans, with which Bouch had planned to cross the Forth at Queensferry. This contract was already let when the fall of the Tay Bridge led to its cancellation some months later. Perhaps it was for the best, since it might have justifiably been dubbed the world's ugliest bridge (despite fierce competition from bridges elsewhere). When Sir Thomas Bouch stood before the three Commissioners who had been instructed by the President of the Board of Trade to inquire into the fall of the Tay Bridge, his faith in his masterpiece remained unshaken. Perhaps these days he would be said to have been in a state of denial.

When he was first called to give evidence on 30 April 1880, he was asked: 'Have you built many large bridges and viaducts?' His proud answer was: 'A great number. I do not suppose anybody has built more.' Slightly boastful, perhaps, but he was fighting for his professional life and the gloves were off.

In the latter half of the last century three full-length books and innumerable articles have been written on the story of the Tay Bridge itself, and yet another, perhaps the best yet for a technical examination of the cause of the lug failures, was published in 2004. The subject is far too vast to be dealt with adequately within the confines of a chapter or two, and Bouch's side of the story will be presented here. Although on occasion he could be his own worst enemy, the devastating condemnation made by Henry Rothery,

Commissioner of Wrecks, who presented the minority report, has gone down in history despite being far from the whole truth. That will never be known.

It was his graphic account of the tragedy, *The High Girders*, by the late John Prebble, that first aroused my interest in Thomas Bouch as far back as 1994. I must put on record here the invaluable help I have received over the last twelve years from the Head Librarian of the Institution of Civil Engineers, Mike Chrimes, and his Archivist, Carol Morgan. No request has been too much trouble, and without their help this book, if it was published at all, would have been very much the poorer. This interest led on to books by the late John Thomas, doyen of Scottish railway historians, which started to fill the gaps in the record. Add to these a brief but informative biography by Professor Alan Earnshaw, published in *Back Track* historical railway periodical. For first-hand information there are the official Minutes of the Public Inquiry held in 1880 running to 580 pages plus appendices. About twenty thousand questions were asked, and by no means were all answered satisfactorily.

To the above sources must be added a short account of the Tay Bridges written by Dr James S. Shipway on behalf of the Institution of Civil Engineers in Scotland, and an admirable short history of *The Fall of the Tay Bridge* by David Swinfen, Professor of History at Dundee University. Most recently, *The Bridge of the Silvery Tay* has appeared from the pen of Dr Peter R. Lewis, a senior lecturer at the Open University. This is likely to remain the definitive history of the tragic event for years to come. I must express my deep indebtedness to all these authors, as well as to many others listed in the Bibliography and Acknowledgements. Above all my gratitude is due to William (Bill) Dow of Carnoustie, who knows more about the Tay Bridge than any man alive, and unstintingly shared his expertise. Lastly I must mention without fail Keith Horne of Ross-on-Wye, who once again has guided me in all matters concerning structural engineering. However, I cannot go without recording my thanks to Professor Roland A. Paxton MBE of Herriot-Watt University, Edinburgh, who offered me every encouragement when I first embarked on this book.

This is not a biography of Thomas Bouch in the usual sense but more a catalogue of his many achievements, most of which are completely forgotten. Perhaps this will allow him a small niche in engineering history to which he is reasonably entitled. He was certainly not the charlatan that many, who should have known better, have claimed. His technical knowledge was acquired the hard way from practical experience, and he was not too proud to seek the help of others when it was needed. Where he stood out from most of his contemporaries was in the boldness and originality of his concepts. For his clients, giving value for money was a paramount consideration.

Unfortunately he was a very private man and left no personal diary or documents which would have shed some light on his personal and family life, but he seems to have been a good husband and father. Little snippets of information are to be found among his office papers deposited in the Scottish National Archives. We know that he took pleasure in acquiring statuary to show that he was a man with artistic tastes. He collected books with a scientific or engineering content.

Sadly, when his health was failing he had to dispose of his guns and fishing tackle. His only photograph shows no ostentatious gold watchchain; a modest man. He is said to have been a lifelong Liberal but never engaged in politics.

Before I sign off it is my pleasure and duty to express my most sincere thanks to my wife, Elizabeth Susan Rapley, for her patience and tolerance while this book has been in preparation.

John Rapley
Bournemouth
31 May 2006

1

THE ORIGINS OF
THE BOUCH FAMILY

The surname of Bouch has for centuries been associated with West Cumberland and still is today, though it is also found in other parts of the country. John Prebble, in his book *The High Girders*, reported that in earlier times a member of the family had been on a pilgrimage and acquired a coat of arms, 'or, on a cross sable five escallop shells apart', which links him to the squirearchy, and it has been suggested that the name is of French origin. Mostly though, in the nineteenth century they were tradesmen, farmers and sailors. The earliest Bouch to appear on the family tree was John Bouch of Old Hale, who married a Martha Benn some time at the beginning of the eighteenth century. The Benns can be traced back before 1500. William Bouch of Aspatria was the son of John and the father of Sir Thomas Bouch.

At the beginning of the nineteenth century, Master Mariner William Bouch owned the brig *Content*, which was mainly engaged in the coastal trade between Barrow and Silloth. His brother, Martin, was master and part owner of the brig *Anne*.

William also had a part-interest in the 246-ton iron brig *Ardent*, registered at Sunderland. William's nephew, Lancelot, became master of the iron ship *Westmorland*, 310 tons and the second largest vessel trading out of Workington. When not at sea, William's home was at Aspatria, where he courted and married his wife, Elizabeth Isobella, probably in 1812. In 1813, with the first of his children already well on the way, and doubtless with encouragement from his new wife, he retired from the sea and moved to a new home at the Ship Inn at Thursby, about 6 miles west of Carlisle. They had hardly settled in before their son, William, was born. A second son, Richard, followed several years later, and on 25 February 1822 Elizabeth was delivered of a third son, Thomas. To complete the family their fourth child was a daughter, Elizabeth Ann, generally known as Ann, who never married and lived at Thursby until her death at the age of eighty-four. She is said to have gained the distinction, rare for a woman in those days, of being described as an ironmaster, though researches into the Cumberland iron trade have so far failed to confirm this.

It has been rumoured that Captain Bouch took William to see the steamships at Workington, and it may have been from this that sprang young William's interest in steam at sea. He was fortunate in attaining an apprenticeship in the Forth Street Works of Robert Stephenson & Co. at Newcastle-upon-Tyne in about 1828. While he was nearing the end of his time there in 1833, the firm was engaged in building a marine engine for the Russian Black Sea Fleet, and this was their first venture into the use of steam. William was offered the opportunity of going out with the engine, to supervise its installation and maintenance and to train the Russian engineers. Eventually he was formally appointed as Chief Engineer of the Black Sea fleet, and received a medal from the Czar. After six years abroad he was happy to return to England in 1839, and his first thought was to set up in business on his own account.

The Formation of Cowans Sheldon of Carlisle

Some time in 1839, on his return from Russia, William Jnr planned to set up in business on his own account and contacted Edward Pattinson Sheldon, who had been a friend since their days together as apprentices at Robert Stephenson's works at Newcastle. There, together with John Cowans, a fellow apprentice, they had been known as 'an irrepressible trio'. In 1842, and again in 1844, all three met at the Ship Inn, no doubt to discuss their possible business venture. They had the blessing of Robert Stephenson, who was noted for his generosity to former apprentices, with a firm proviso that they did not set up in competition.

Meanwhile, to keep the wolf from the door, William applied for a vacancy for an experienced assistant in the Shildon Works of Timothy Hackworth, who was under contract to the Stockton & Darlington to maintain their fleet of locomotives. Hackworth had ambitions to work independently, and in 1841 he set up a new factory at Shildon, which he called the Soho Works. William was promoted to Locomotive Superintendent by the S&D, and he remained a faithful servant of the company for the next thirty-five years, retiring to the gentler climate of Weymouth in 1875. Sadly, he was not to enjoy his retirement for long, and died on 19 January 1876. He left a widow, Jane, but no children. After ensuring provision for Jane during her lifetime, he left the bulk of his estate to his brother Thomas, for the two brothers had always been very close.

William Bouch had entered the service of the S&D in 1840, and after he became Locomotive Superintendent in 1841 he was no longer able to take an active part in the partnership, but instead delegated his day-to-day responsibilities to Thomas, who in due course acquired the title of Manager, while still working full-time with Larmer. William remained senior partner, and in 1843/4 took a lease on the Woodbank Works, which he assigned to James Cowans in 1846. At about the same period Cowans acquired the lease of Woodbank House and Farm for his own occupation, and to help feed his employees. By 1852 they were outgrowing the Woodbank Works and took a financial interest in the Darlington Forge Co., and the following year all forge work was transferred there. In 1857 they acquired the St Nicholas Works in Carlisle. Until their deaths, William and Thomas remained as sleeping partners

Of the middle brother, Richard, very little is known. He obtained a clerical post in the department of Joseph Pease, Treasurer of the S&D, and the world's first railway treasurer. Somewhat out of character for a sober Quaker and Victorian man of business, Joseph was described as the life and soul of any party. From 1832-1841 he was Liberal MP for South Durham. Among many developments he founded the town of Middlesbrough on 500 acres of what was then described as a dismal swamp. Richard Bouch occupied his post until his early death in 1847.

Growing Up at Thursby: the Early Years

In 1813, when Captain William Bouch and his wife settled in Thursby, it was no doubt typical of a hundred other Cumberland villages, but since all inland transport in the county was by road, its situation on a main road avoided isolation.

Thursby Parish, including the village itself and several outlying hamlets, had a total population of about 500 persons, of whom about 350 actually lived in the village.

A recent view of the Ship Inn at Thursby, which was taken over by the newly married Captain William Bouch and his wife Elizabeth in 1813. Two centuries on, the building has probably changed little from how the Bouch family knew it as children.

St Andrew's church which served the parish of Thursby, *c.*1836. Although Captain William Bouch was married at Aspatria before taking over the Ship Inn, the four Bouch children were baptised here

Left: William Bouch, 1813–1876. He was the eldest brother of Sir Thomas Bouch. Apprenticed to Robert Stephenson & Co. at Newcastle, he spent six years with the Russian Black Fleet, then with Timothy Hackworth at Shildon, before becoming Locomotive Superintendent of the Stockton & Darlington Railway until 1875.

Below, left and right: John Cowans and Edward Sheldon, former Stephenson apprentices, enlisted the help of William and Thomas Bouch to set up their engineering works at Woodbank near Carlisle, which eventually became Cowans & Sheldon, the internationally famous crane makers

Sir Wastel Brisco Bt of Crofton Hall was the principal landowner, and was actively engaged in improving his estate, unlike many other landowners in Cumberland who lacked the necessary capital. Possibly as a result the population had increased by nearly 50% in the twenty years after 1801. There were the usual rural craftsmen, a boot and shoe maker, a shopkeeper, a blacksmith, a joiner and cartwright, as well as a corn miller and grocer, while William Bouch at the Ship Inn and Jane Williamson at the Horse and Groom were listed as victuallers. Since the village is on the main road between Carlisle, Wigston and Cockermouth, they probably enjoyed a welcome passing trade. George Brown, victualler of The Greyhound at Micklethwaite, 3 miles from Thursby, was less fortunately situated.

The spiritual needs of the parishioners were served by the Church of St Andrew, which appears at that date to have faced no competition from dissenting chapels. Methodism must have passed Thursby by. Doubtless the Bouch family were regular attendees at St Andrew's and the children were all baptised there. The parish was served both by a vicar, the Revd William Tomkyns Briggs MA, but also by a curate, the Revd William Ford, the reason being that the vicar had duties as a lecturer in Carlisle for six months in the year. Both clergymen resided in the village. When Thomas Bouch moved to Edinburgh he, and in due course his family, attended the Episcopal Church of Scotland, which is in communion with the Anglican Church, at Holy Trinity, Dean Bridge, and it was there that his funeral service was held in 1880. Since then the juggernaut of progress has rolled on and, deserted by its congregation, the church now houses an electricity substation.

The village of Thursby lay on the estate of Sir Mastel Brisco Bt and most of the village housing, and possibly the Ship Inn itself, would have been rented from the Brisco Estate. Of the seventy-five houses, none was occupied by more than one family, which suggests some degree of modest prosperity. Inevitably there would have been poverty, but the landlord's programme of improvements had led to a growth in agricultural employment. Around 1822, when Thomas Bouch was born, Thursby seems to have been a small but growing and well-ordered community.

In the matter of education Thursby was relatively fortunate. When Thomas Tomlinson, a native of Thursby, died in North Carolina in 1798, he left an endowment of £374. Under the trusteeship of Sir Wastel Brisco this produced an annual income of £17 14s. Ten poor children were educated for 10s per year while the better-off like the Bouch family paid £1. There were no rich pickings for the schoolmaster, Joseph Hannah, but he was married and brought up a son, also Joseph, who, after returning from college, became his father's assistant. Doubtless with a cow in the byre, a pig in the sty and a good vegetable garden they managed as well as most. The curriculum was fairly basic and adapted to the needs of the pupils, most of whom would spend their lives in agriculture or domestic service. There was industry, coal and iron-ore mining, metalliferous mining and stone and slate quarrying though as yet on a small scale until the arrival of the railways. The Maryport & Carlisle Railway opened a station at Curthwaite, about a mile south of Thursby, in May 1843.

All four of the Bouch children learned their 3Rs at the village school in Thursby, and learned them well at the hands of Joseph Hannah and his son of the same name. Education in the early 1800s was very much a hit-or-miss affair depending on where you lived and what your parents could afford to pay. So-called free grammar schools were often endowed to teach Latin and Greek to poor scholars. Anything else had to be paid for. Only those parents who could afford a private school of varying quality might hope for a broad education such as Robert Stephenson was given at Dr Bruce's Academy in Newcastle. For the unlucky ones this was the era of Dotheboys Hall. At that time Cumberland was declared to be the poorest county in England, and although the Church of England was the principal provider of primary schooling it could only build and run schools where local funds or endowments were available.

It was in this small and peaceful country village that the Bouch children grew up. Thomas showed little enthusiasm for the work of the classroom until one special day. Before then fishing, guddling trout in the becks, or shooting or swimming in the sea at Allonby were far closer to his heart, and when harmless mischief was afoot he was something of a ringleader. Joseph Hannah Junior had acquired an interest in scientific studies, or Natural Philosophy as it was then known. Casting about for a new subject to interest his pupils, he gave them a lesson on how to make water run uphill. Something in this caught Thomas's imagination and, as the younger Joseph Hannah reported later when attending Thomas's funeral, thereafter Thomas seized upon any technical books that he could find in his master's small library.

Above left: Edward Pease of Darlington. He developed various industrial interests in north Durham, and could rightfully claim to be the 'Father of the Railways', as distinct from colliery tramways, in that part of the country, starting with the Stockton & Darlington.

Above right: Joseph Pease, Treasurer of the Stockton & Darlington Railway and the world's first Railway Treasurer. Until his premature death, Richard Bouch, the middle son of Captain William Bouch, worked in Joseph Pease's office.

About the time in 1835 that Thomas would normally have left the village school, the Headship of the Academy School in Abbey Street, Carlisle, fell vacant and the younger Hannah applied for the post and was duly appointed. With his father's encouragement Thomas continued his education in Carlisle, lodging with his schoolmaster's family during the week and walking home at weekends. No details of the curriculum remain, but it is interesting to compare the range of subjects taught at that period at Whalley Grammar School, not far away in North Lancashire. Naturally at that time in history Holy Scripture headed the list, followed by reading, writing, and arithmetic, mensuration and land surveying, Latin, French, German, and Greek, natural science, chemistry, mechanics and drawing (freehand, model, mechanical and shading), elocution, and book-keeping etc. If Joseph Hannah could inculcate even half of these subjects into Thomas it can fairly be said that the lad received an unusually comprehensive education for the time.

Everything seemed to be going smoothly when the sudden and unexpected death of Captain Bouch in 1838 threw the family into confusion. By then only Thomas and his sister, Elizabeth Ann, were left at home. The disconsolate widow decided to carry on running The Ship with her daughter's help, but it was clear that from now on Thomas would have to make his own way in the world. He was, after all, now sixteen and ready for an apprenticeship. Thomas was found a place with a Liverpool firm of mechanical engineers. A branch of the Bouch family resided in Liverpool, they too were seafarers, and Thomas was probably looked after by them, hence the choice of Liverpool. Despite this the job did not prove a success, whether through home-sickness, for it was the first time he had left home, or because the grim working conditions were intolerable to a country boy used to roaming the open fells. Thomas was soon back home in Thursby when a great stroke of good fortune intervened.

From the south the railway had reached Lancaster, and the next stage in developing what was to become the West Coast main line was to penetrate the mountainous area that lay between Lancaster and Carlisle. This was a formidable undertaking and a formidable engineer, Joseph Locke, was given the task. By 1840 Locke was joined by his lifetime partner, John Errington, and this became one of the most fruitful associations in railway history. The initial survey was carried out from an office in Carlisle, where a George Larmer was put in charge. Larmer was a man with considerable experience gained on the Newcastle & Carlisle Railway, which had been opened throughout in 1838 after delays due to strong opposition from local landowners. Much of the land over Shap was almost worthless, and here the owners proved more amenable. It was amazing though how land values shot up when a railway surveyor was sighted. Larmer advertised for an assistant, and Joseph Hannah put Thomas's name forward as a likely candidate, giving him a good reference. With this backing young Thomas was duly appointed, and over the following four years received a thorough grounding in railway surveying which would stand him in good stead for the rest of his life.

It would appear that this two-man band was left to survey the whole 69 miles, and it took them the best part of four years, working in all seasons over some of the roughest ground in Cumbria. No doubt they had the assistance of a pair of chainmen and a staff holder or two, but these men and their ponies, one each for the surveyors and a third to carry the heavy surveying gear, had to face all that the weather could throw at them, though of course there was much work in the office in Carlisle to occupy them in winter.

The Lancaster & Carlisle Railway

As early as the end of January 1836, Joseph Locke had completed and published a report entitled 'London & Glasgow Railway through Lancashire'. This was a remarkable effort for he was still only thirty years of age and heavily engaged elsewhere. One proposal was a line through Windermere and Ambleside, but not only was this fiercely opposed, not least by William Wordsworth, but it would have involved very hard going. The scheme was quickly dropped. The alternatives were through Longsleddale to Haweswater, involving a lengthy tunnel, something that Locke abhorred, or alternatively through Lonsdale and over Shap. The report was shelved and in 1838 George Stephenson's advice was sought. Fearful as always of gradients exceeding about 1:300 he advised a coastal route through Furness and along the West Cumberland coastline to meet the planned Maryport & Carlisle Railway, also a Stephenson project. This involved not only crossing both the wide Kent and Duddon Estuaries, but also resulted in a much longer route. Although this line was eventually built to serve the developing iron industry, and was opened in 1857 by James Brunlees, it has always remained merely a secondary route.

The Prime Minister of the day, Sir Robert Peel, appointed a Commission consisting of Sir Frederick Smith, the earliest Government Railway Inspector, and Professor Peter Barlow from the Royal Engineers at Chatham, to investigate possible railway routes to Scotland. Their report, published in May 1840, was non-committal, and George Larmer was instructed to do a quick visual survey of the two competing routes through the fells. He reported on 3 July, favouring the line through the Lune Gorge with a slight detour near Grayrigg which avoided any need for tunnelling. Since the proposed line passed near Lord Lonsdale's residence at Lowther Castle, he offered strong objections, which delayed progress for nearly two and a half years. Meanwhile Larmer and Bouch were engaged in completing the Parliamentary survey, and the Royal Assent was finally given in June 1844.

Woodbank House, near Carlisle, was bought by Cowans & Sheldon when they started their engineering business in the adjacent former textile mill. The farmhouse offered accommodation for themselves, and the farm provided food for their employees.

The contract for the 69 miles was awarded to Thomas Brassey, and was the largest single contract ever awarded up to that date. Locke knew Brassey's capabilities, and that the work would be in safe hands. Work commenced in July 1844, and George Larmer was appointed Resident Engineeer, but although he begged Bouch to stay on, the young surveyor decided that he needed to broaden his experience and resigned. Larmer wrote to Joseph Hannah at Carlisle, asking if he had another pupil of equal ability to Bouch to fill his place. It so happened at that time that James Falshaw, principal assistant to George Leather Junior of Leeds, applied for a post as engineer on the Lancaster & Carlisle, and Bouch moved to Leeds as assistant to Leather. Falshaw later had a successful and profitable career as a railway contractor, mostly in Scotland, eventually becoming Chairman of the North British Railway and Lord Provost of Edinburgh, where his path and Bouch's crossed once again.

Life with George Leather at Leeds

There were two George Leathers, father and son. Leather Senior (1748–1818) was a civil engineer of the old school of canal builders, but like most of the early engineers was willing, when the need arose, to turn his hand to anything. Few civil engineers in those days could afford to be specialists. He was appointed engineer of the Surrey Iron Railway, surveyed by Willam Jessop, another veteran of the canal age, and sanctioned by Parliament in 1801. The railway (in fact a plateway) ran from the Thames at Wandsworth to Croydon, and is generally considered to be the world's first public railway in the sense that it had been authorised by an Act of Parliament. George Junior went to work as his father's assistant and thus received a very early grounding in railway construction. In due course he followed his father as engineer of the Aire & Calder Canal, and designed the impressive cast-iron arch aqueduct for the canal at Stanley Ferry, where it crosses the Calder, with a clear span of 155ft. He became known as a builder of several major cast-iron bridges across the Aire in the Leeds area, and designed a four-span toll bridge to cross the Trent at Dunhan, the only road crossing of the Trent between Gainsborough and Newark.

Joseph Locke belonged to the Great Triumvirate of early railway engineers, together with I.K. Brunel and Robert Stephenson. He engineered the Lancaster & Carlisle Railway, where Thomas Bouch learnt railway surveying under George Larmer.

All these were based on cast-iron arches somewhat resembling the Sydney Harbour Bridge in appearance.

Although a provincial, and often looked down upon by his London-based colleagues, Leather Junior was regarded in his prime as one of the most outstanding engineers in the country. In the 1830s he was joined by his nephew, John Wignall Leather (1810-1887). When Thomas Bouch joined his staff in 1844 George Leather was fifty-seven and past his prime, delegating much of the work to his nephew, who later became a distinguished civil engineer in his own right.

In 1838 Leather had been appointed by the Holme Reservoirs Commissioners to oversee the construction of several earth-fill gravity dams. With the assistance of Falshaw these were duly completed, but the Bilberry Dam was a source of trouble from the beginning, probably due to George Leather's inexperience in this form of structure. When Bouch started he was involved in attempts to solve the problems at Bilberry, but with the Railway Mania gaining momentum he no doubt thought that railways were where the future lay. In fact he was well away from it, for in the middle of the night on 5 February 1852 the dam failed. Eighty-one people died in the ensuing flood and 310 properties were destroyed or seriously damaged. The Commissioners were held to blame, but as a corporate body they were exempt from a charge of manslaughter. This unfortunate affair effectively finished George Leather's career, though it resulted in no prosecutions.

The Victorians were inured to catastrophes on land, sea and underground, and the Bilberry Dam failure was a nine-day wonder. Twelve years after Bilberry, the much larger Dale Dyke Dam, 9 miles west of Sheffield, failed even more disastrously, and remains the most catastrophic structural failure in the history of British civil engineering. The engineer involved was John Towlerton Leather (1804-1885). On this occasion nearly 250 lives were lost, and innumerable properties damaged or destroyed downstream as far as Sheffield. Since all the dead were from the labouring classes, not possessing votes, there was little pressure on the Home Secretary for an Inquiry. Only five witnesses were heard at the Coroner's Inquest. The jury attributed the deaths to accidental drowning, no one was held responsible, but they recommended that Parliament should legislate on dam safety. Only sixty-six years later was this finally achieved. This is to put in perspective the enormous public outcry over the loss of some seventy-five lives at the Tay Bridge fifteen years afterwards, and the major Public Inquiry which followed.

Learning His Profession on the Wear Valley Railway

On 31 July 1845 an Act was passed for the construction of a railway 10¾ miles in length from Wear Valley Junction on the Bishop Auckland & Weardale Railway to a temporary terminus at Frosterley. This was known as the Wear Valley Railway, and Thomas Bouch was appointed as an assistant engineer under John Dixon of the Stockton & Darlington. No doubt William Bouch, now working for the S&D, put in a good word for his brother. There were grand plans to extend through Alston to Carlisle, but the financial fallout from the Railway Mania put paid to further development and it was 1895 before the further 9¼ miles to Wearhead was opened. By the time the line opened in August 1847 Bouch had received a good grounding in railway construction to go with his surveyor's training.

His employment on the Stockton & Darlington brought Bouch into contact with the Pease family. Although originally engaged in the wool trade and as bankers, they exerted great influence on the development of heavy industry in South Durham, and as Quakers their high standards of business ethics made them widely respected. Edward Pease (1767–1858) and his two sons, Joseph and Henry, were involved with railway development in Durham from the early days of the tramroads, and in due course into railways, Joseph being described as the first railway treasurer. Henry Pease took on his father's mantle and played a major part in railway development in the North-East of England. While the popular description of George Stephenson as 'father of the steam locomotive' is highly controversial, Edward Pease had a far better claim to have been 'the father of railways'. Another of his five sons, Isaac, tragically died on the morning of the opening of the Stockton & Darlington Railway, while two other sons were engaged in other aspects of their father's business empire. But for all their wealth the Pease family lived modestly, as befitted members of the Society of Friends, and put on no airs or graces.

At the age of twenty-four Bouch, the country publican's son, still had a few rough edges, but social contact with Edward Pease and his sons offered him an opportunity to remedy this. Quakers were traditionally regarded as being dull but worthy, but Joseph was reported to be 'full of go and the life and soul of the party'. In 1832 that most estimable of men became the first Quaker Member of Parliament. Richard wrote:

> My dear brother Tom,
> With pleasure I received your letter, thankfully acknowledging its contents, but I am sorry to learn that you are spending your time unprofitably now that it is so valuable, and I urge you to neglect no opportunity of cultivating the air of becoming an accepted gentleman and embrace every privilege of mixing with good society.

This excellent advice was taken to heart, very much to his future advantage when it came to negotiating with landowners like the Duke of Cleveland and Boards of Directors, and of course when appearing before Parliamentary Committees.

Almost gone was the Cumbrian accent; Thomas Bouch was now a gentleman!

Having seen the position of Manager of the Edinburgh & Northern Railway advertised, Bouch thought that he had nothing to lose by applying, and he was encouraged in this by John Dixon. Although the S&D would be sorry to lose him, they had little development in hand and they did not wish to stand in the way of his advancement. Edward Pease came to hear of Bouch's plans, and generously gave him an excellent testimonial. So it was off to Edinburgh for an interview.

2

THE EDINBURGH, PERTH
& DUNDEE RAILWAY

The first railway to penetrate the north side of Edinburgh was the Edinburgh, Leith & Newhaven, which received its Act on 13 August 1836. From Canonmills, in the valley of the Water of Leith, it tunnelled beneath the New Town on a rising gradient of 1:27 to emerge in a deep cutting immediately south of Princes Street, where the Waverley Market now stands. The engineers were Grainger and Miller, Scotland's leading consultants in the early days of railway development, and noted for the high quality of their masonry structures. Their assistant engineer was young William Paterson of Perth, who had particular responsibility for the Scotland Street Tunnel. Some forty years later, as he approached retirement, the same William Paterson would be chosen by Bouch to be his resident engineer on the Tay Bridge. As was the case with so many early schemes, lack of money caused the Leith branch to be abandoned for the time being in 1839, though the main line was completed as far as Trinity Station.

The Scotland Street Tunnel

The principal engineering feature at the Edinburgh end of the Edinburgh, Perth and Dundee Railway (EP&D) was the tunnel which connected Canal Street Station to the locomotive-operated section between Canonmills and Granton Harbour. It was constructed by the Edinburgh, Leith & Newhaven Railway under its Act of 13 August 1836. The Company engineer was the much-respected Thomas Grainger, G. Buchanan was the resident engineer, and the assistant engineer was young William Paterson. He was one of that band of hardworking middle engineering management who contributed so greatly to the success of the railway system, but who received little of the public acclaim accorded to their masters. At Stirling he supervised the building of an iron lattice girder bridge over the Forth for the Stirling & Dunfermline Railway, which ran side by side with Joseph Locke's creaking timber arches of the Scottish Central Railway. At Perth he was responsible for the construction and development over many years of the Joint Station. It was there that Thomas Bouch found him, and offered him the poisoned chalice of the post of resident engineer on the Tay Bridge. It was to lead to his death after the fall of the bridge.

1,052 yards in length on a continuous gradient of 1:27, it still exists, though out of use for many years, and runs from below the present Waverley Market down to the northern end of Scotland Street, where a handsome stone portal, built by Ross & Mitchell, is still to be seen. As far down as Drummond Place and Dublin Street, the ground was firm, but under Scotland Street it degenerated into clay and sand which gave rise to concern regarding the houses on either side. The Company was under a legal obligation to purchase any house damaged, but in the event this never occurred. The only serious accident was an ingress of water under Dublin Street in November 1844 when four men were drowned.

Almost from the beginning a decision was reached to use continuous rope haulage in the tunnel, although the Act permitted the use of locomotives providing that they consumed their own smoke. Two 40hp beam haulage engines were ordered from Hawthorn of Newcastle. Trains (without locomotives) were hauled up to Canal Street and descended to Scotland Street controlled by brake trucks and the use of wheel sprags. The hemp haulage rope was 6ins in diameter, and had to be replaced at regular intervals at an average maintenance cost of £500 a year. No broken ropes were ever reported, and the tunnel was finally closed to rail traffic on 2 March 1868 after the opening of Bouch's new line from Waverley via Abbeyhill and Leith Walk. Canal Street Station was then closed and Granton trains ran from Waverley. Demolition of the old EP&D Station then allowed a northward expansion of Waverley and a long-overdue revision of the layout, including a new glazed iron roof designed by Bouch, and the old masonry overbridge where the railway had penetrated the 'Little Mound' was demolished and a new iron bridge built according to a design by Bouch.

When Thomas Bouch arrived as the new Manager at Canal Street early in 1849, the tunnel was in regular use, although the descending journey was rather a nerve-shattering experience and many travellers may have decided to embark at Scotland Street.

A watercolour painted in 1847 by Joseph Ebsworth. It is the view looking eastwards from the recently completed Scott Monument. Princes Street is on the left, with the Little Mound in the foreground. Canal Street Station on its cramped site can be seen on the right, and the North British Railway is on the extreme right, beyond Canal Street on its arches.

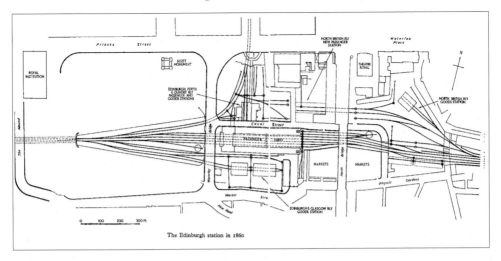

The Edinburgh station in 1860

The Edinburgh, or North Bridge, Station about 1860, showing the Canal Street Station and its very cramped layout. The bottleneck caused by the tunnel under the Mound was duplicated to the east by the Calton Tunnel.

One of Bouch's first actions was to dismiss the driver of the stationary engine for breach of regulations. Although goods wagons could he handled by a short siding from the Edinburgh & Glasgow, from where a horse took over, the effectiveness of the brake trucks strictly limited the loads that could be handled as, for that matter, did the need to tranship everything at Granton. Even with the opening of the train ferries in 1850, the tunnel remained a formidable bottleneck. Bouch could see that a line, bypassing the tunnel, was essential, yet it took until 1868 for this to be achieved after the rebuilding of Waverley. On 28 August 1861 the Caledonian was able to offer a goods service to Granton Harbour by a branch from its main line at Slateford, and this must have taken away much of the NBR goods traffic until the 1868 diversion was built.

For many years after it closed the tunnel was used for growing mushrooms, but this ceased in 1917. In more recent years it was used for the storage of cars, but today it lies empty. A section under Princes Street was used at one time as an emergency control room, with access from Waverley.

Down to the Ferries at Granton

Initially the line was planned to run to a station close to the sea at Trinity, on the western edge of the fishing village of Newhaven, from where it was a short walk to the Chain Pier and ferries across the Forth to Burntisland and various small harbours in Fife, a distance of about 5 miles of open water, subject in winter to fierce storms. In 1898 the Chain Pier was finally destroyed in an unusually severe storm, but it had long since been out of use for regular crossings. Hardly had work begun on the railway than the Duke of Buccleuch commenced building a commodious harbour at Granton, little more than half a mile west of the Chain Pier. A new Act was obtained to extend the railway, by this time renamed the Edinburgh, Leith & Granton, to a station on what later became the Centre Pier at Granton after the harbour was extended westwards. While the harbour was opened by Queen Victoria on 31 August 1842, it took the railway until 19 February 1846 to actually reach Granton. The long delay may be explained in part by the generally chaotic state of the management at that time, and the financial after-effects of the Railway Mania which restricted the availability of capital.

The west end of Waverley Station about 1860, photographed by George Washington Wilson. The cramped layout is obvious and at that time there were only two lines through to Haymarket. The spur to Canal Street is visible on the left in the foreground.

Waverley Station about 1870 after the first rebuilding when Thomas Bouch designed a new roof and the new Waverley Bridge in the foreground.

Trinity Junction, where the new 1868 line from Waverley via Leith Walk, coming in from the right, joined the old line from the Scotland Street Tunnel. This view is looking north towards Trinity Station and Granton.

Trinity Junction looking south to Scotland Street goods yard. The new line from Waverley bypassing the Scotland Street Tunnel is coming in on the left. The nearest bridge carries the Caledonian line from Saughton to Leith North Station.

The Edinburgh & Northern line in Fife picked up its traffic from the ferries at Burntisland Harbour, and provided connections to Perth by courtesy of a short run over Scottish Central tracks from Hilton Junction into what became the Joint Station, erected under the supervision of William Paterson. Ferryport-on-Craig (soon changed to Tayport) was the harbour for the Tay ferries to Broughty Ferry and Dundee. In June 1847 the Edinburgh & Northern acquired the Forth ferries and on 27 July took over the ailing Edinburgh, Leith & Granton Railway, which became the southern outpost of the Edinburgh & Northern Railway. In mid-1847 there was another change of name to the E,P&D. In spite of its grand name it had no line of its own into Perth, and none at all into Dundee until the opening of the Tay Bridge some thirty years later. Its troubles were far from over, and in desperation advertisements were placed for a new General Manager to oversee the commercial operations. Meanwhile, Thomas Grainger remained for a while as consulting engineer.

Bouch had profited greatly from his years with the Stockton & Darlington Railway, but by 1848 the heady days of its early expansion had given way to a period of consolidation in line with the financial aftermath of the Railway Mania. Bouch was naturally anxious to expand his interests, and, as was the custom of the period, it was accepted as normal for him to move on and seek promotion, leaving no hard feelings behind. He had enjoyed a good grounding in surveying with George Larmer, and in actual railway construction with the S&D, under its esteemed engineer John Dixon. He had also established excellent relations with the Pease family of Quakers, who dominated the early days of the S&D. In future years he would be called back by the S&D to undertake special projects.

Thus it would seem that at the age of twenty-six Bouch had much to offer a prospective employer, and when he decided to apply for the post of Manager on the Edinburgh & Northern Railway, as it continued to call itself, he could imagine himself as 'master of his own ship', just as his father had been, instead of only an assistant engineer. Another effect of the end of the Railway Mania was to increase greatly the number of applicants for any post which fell vacant. Such was the demand in 1845 that almost any fool with a smattering of elementary surveying could find employment and describe himself as a railway surveyor, but conditions had changed drastically three years later. Bouch found himself one among 105 applicants, and it is almost certain that a very warm letter of recommendation from Henry Pease swung the balance in his favour. To a prospective employer Quakers could be relied upon to tell the unvarnished truth.

The Journey to Edinburgh

The Maryport & Carlisle Railway had opened in 1843, and there was a station a short distance south of Thursby, but called Curthwaite after a hamlet nearby. Thus it was that one day early in January 1849 Bouch picked up a train to Carlisle from Curthwaite, or very possibly walked into town as he had done so many times before. At Carlisle he found himself a seat in an unheated railway carriage (steam heating on the Caledonian was unknown until 1883), with his luggage safely stowed in the guard's van and a one-way first class ticket to Edinburgh in his pocket. Though the Caledonian route from Carstairs to Edinburgh had opened earlier in 1846, money had run low, and instead of the magnificent station designed by Sir William Tite, after a foundation stone had been laid with great ceremony by the Lord Provost of Edinburgh, Bouch found his journey ended in a mere wooden shanty. When money was short it was the passenger accommodation that usually suffered, even on the pioneering London & Birmingham Railway. At that time and for many years to come, the shared Edinburgh & Glasgow and NBR station at North Bridge was equally and justifiably the subject of criticism. Railway passengers were too often treated as second class citizens.

Abbeyhill Station, the first on the new line from Waverley to Trinity Junction which made the Scotland Street Tunnel redundant and allowed the closure of Canal Street Station and the northward expansion of Waverley to take the new traffic.

The former Trinity Station, now forming two houses. This was the first terminus of the Edinburgh, Leith & Newhaven Railway and was within easy walking distance of the Trinity Chain Pier for travellers crossing the Forth or taking pleasure trips.

The station on Granton middle pier built by the Edinburgh, Perth & Dundee Railway. It was a short walk to the ferries to Burntisland. The former slipway for Bouch's flying bridge was behind the line of trucks on the right.

Arrival at Canal Street Station

On his arrival in Edinburgh after a cold and uncomfortable journey, Bouch doubtless looked around for a meal and a bed for the night, before finding his way next morning to the Canal Street Station – the Edinburgh Station as the Company still proudly declared it, arguing that they were in business before the other companies arrived in the city.

Canal Street has long disappeared from the street map of Edinburgh, but in 1849 it still ran eastwards from what later became Waverley Bridge and approximately where the north carriage entrance of the modern station now lies. The name Canal Street calls for some explanation, for there had never been a canal in the vicinity. It would appear that many years before there had been an ill-conceived and long defunct scheme to extend the Union Canal from its terminal at Port Hopetoun at Fountainbridge, eastwards through the valley of the former North Loch, and then turning north through the deep cleft in a ridge of rock at the foot of Calton Hill now occupied by Calton Road. A terminal basin was to be built in Greenside Place, an area noted for its unreliable geological conditions, and eventually extended down to Leith. Canal Street was roughly on the line of the planned canal, and so the name survived.

Fortified by a good Scottish breakfast, Bouch buttoned up his greatcoat, jammed his stovepipe hat firmly down on his head, and made his way along Princes Street in the half-light of an Edinburgh winter morning, admiring as he went the fine hotels, houses and shops, and the already busy traffic. Carlisle, Darlington, and not even Newcastle had anything more imposing to offer. Passing the two-year-old monument to Sir Walter Scott, already darkening from the smoke of a thousand chimneys, he turned right on to Canal Street and descended the incline to the modest headquarters of what was now the Edinburgh, Perth & Dundee Railway. Little did he think then that twenty-five years later he would become engineer for the new Waverley Bridge and the roof for the redevelopment of Waverley Station. The EP&D was administered from Edinburgh although by far the greater part of its mileage lay over the water in Fife.

The 'Edinburgh Station' was a rather mean little two-storied structure, there was no room for anything better, with two short platforms and a number of sidings accessed by turntables. It is unlikely that it ever saw a locomotive except when a sharply curved spur was used to transfer goods wagons from the Edinburgh & Glasgow line. From his previous visit for an interview, Bouch knew what to expect and realised that there was little scope for improvement now that it was hemmed in on the south side of Canal Street by the North Bridge Station (Waverley after 1854) of the North British Railway, shared with the Edinburgh & Glasgow Railway, which had been the first to arrive on the scene. All carriage and wagon movements within the EP&D Station area relied on horse power.

The inability of the Canal Street Station to extend southwards rose from an agreement between the first two companies to arrive to share out the available land. The Edinburgh & Glasgow stole a march on the smaller company by taking over land south of Canal Street, and offered in exchange extra land northwards which demanded heavy excavation. This resulted in a most inconvenient layout with short platforms, and sidings fanning out to either side. The EP&D claimed £60,000 in compensation and eventually the matter went to arbitration by R.B. Dockray of the LNWR and T.H. Bertram of the GWR, who had been chief assistant to I.K. Brunel. Dockray's comments in his private diary were very much to the point:

> I never saw a station more wretchedly contrived. The space is much cramped and so laid out that I don't wonder that they complain of insufficient accommodation. The goods and passengers are so huddled together that it is a matter of great labour to separate them.

A compromise plan was finally agreed but there was no mention of compensation. Bouch had to do his best with things as he found them.

Above and below: The 'flying bridge' in use at Burntisland. This photograph was probably taken near high water since the deck of the ferry is quite high. One of the Company's passenger ferries, the *John Stirling* is just visible on the right of the picture below.

Bouch's 'flying bridge' at Granton. The slipway shown still exists. This was probably the first ever wagon ferry, and passenger coaches and locomotives were not carried. Passengers were tolerated but no accommodation was provided.

A wagon ferry at Granton

Bouch's 'flying bridge' at Granton loading wagons onto the deck of one of the ferries at Burntisland. The apparatus could be moved up or down the slipway according to the state of the tide, while the drawbridge accommodated the changes in the height of the ferry deck above water.

Opposite above: The new and much larger ferry *Leviathan*, introduced with the construction of the 'flying bridge', which plied between Granton and Burntisland twenty-hour hours a day in all weathers. There was no accommodation for passengers for the half-hour journey

One of the smaller ferry boats, *Carrie*. She was adapted for rail traffic by laying rails on her deck. As traffic grew these were gradually phased out, and faster boats with passenger accommodation were introduced on both crossings.

An artist's impression of great activity in Granton Harbour. The West Pier has been completed. The larger vessels are probably members of the whaling fleet. The ferries to Burntisland ran until the opening of the Forth Bridge in 1890.

The northern end of the Scotland Street Tunnel, probably taken shortly after closure in 1868/9. Rails, platforms and the corrugated-iron shanty still remained. The handsome tunnel portal exists today. This was where William Paterson, resident engineer on the Tay Bridge, learnt his profession.

Scotland Street Station just prior to closure to all traffic. The tunnel in the foreground to Waverley had closed a century earlier and for many years housed a thriving mushroom-growing industry. The site is now a recreation ground.

The former Scotland Street Station almost a century after passenger traffic had ceased. Looking north towards Granton, the handsome Grainger & Miller tunnel portal was typical of their high standard of design and workmanship.

Advent of a New Broom

It was symptomatic of the disorganisation of the EP&D that Bouch found news of his imminent arrival had not been passed to the station foreman, and that as a result no provision had been made for his office. The previous Manager, Francis Cockshott, five years younger than Bouch, was probably lacking in experience and authority, and received little help from his directors. Eventually both he and the locomotive superintendent resigned, and the assistant locomotive engineer was dismissed for misconduct. Bills were remaining unpaid and debts were increasing month by month. The builder of the chimney for the steam engines which drew trains up the Scotland Street Tunnel was complaining bitterly that he had been kept waiting two years for his money, and he was far from the only victim. Only the amalgamation of the E&N with the EP&D had saved the day financially, but Bouch had to steer this rudderless ship as best he could. Wasting no time, he tackled the demoralised labour force. There were of course many good men, lacking only leadership, but others were drunken, incompetent, impertinent and altogether ill-disciplined. This was no longer going to be tolerated.

Bouch was not by nature a hard man, but these were times when instant hiring and firing was accepted by both men and management. Bouch had to keep the railway running and could not simply fire the lot and start afresh, so men willing to admit the error of their ways were offered a second chance. Some though had erred too far and received short shrift. The word soon spread around that the new Manager would stand no nonsense. At his first meeting with the Board on 20 February 1849, two days before his twenty-seventh birthday, Bouch reported that Porter Horsburgh at Canal Street had been summarily discharged for being drunk, fighting and extorting money from passengers. The services of another three men were dispensed with for irregular attendance and neglect of duty. This was but a start, for before long, over in Fife, Bouch sacked seventy-seven workers, but doubled the number of inspectors. It was money well spent and improvements in the service quickly followed. The Directors expressed their satisfaction and Bouch found himself promoted to engineer and Manager with an additional salary of £500 a year. It was an encouraging start.

In the matter of locomotive power Bouch found that all were almost new, totalling twenty-four in number, and had been supplied by R. & W. Hawthorn of Newcastle in 1847 and 1848. Four intended for light express passenger work had a 2-2-2 wheel arrangement with 6ft driving wheels, while ten 0-4-2s with 5ft coupled wheels were for more general duties. Heavy goods traffic was served by ten 0-6-0 coupled locomotives with 4ft 6in driving wheels and somewhat larger cylinders. These at least, if properly maintained, could handle all the traffic offered. Coke for the locomotives was supplied by a range of coke ovens at Pettycur in Fife, belonging to the Marlowhill Coke Co. These lasted until about 1870 when coal-burning locomotives became the norm, and they were then redeveloped as a saltworks, of which many had long existed on both sides of the Forth Estuary due to the easy availability of ample, cheap coal.

Even though their route was longer, the Caledonian offered fierce competition for passenger and goods traffic to Perth, Dundee and Aberdeen, and with no need for ferry crossings it was as fast, and far safer and more comfortable in bad weather.

Like most railways of the period, profitability lay in goods traffic and passengers were regarded as an unprofitable nuisance, given to complaining and making life difficult for railway management. The little steamers which the company ran as ferries across the Firth of Forth lacked any covered accommodation for passengers. Conditions at Dundee were little better though the privately owned ferry boats catered for a well-to-do commuter traffic to and from Dundee and Broughty Ferry to serve Newport and Tayport on the south bank. Businessmen who had built their mansions at Newport provided a steady flow of business, but if the EP&D was ever to develop a worthwhile goods traffic urgent improvements were unavoidable.

The Chain Pier at Trinity on the Forth near the fishing village of Newhaven. For years this carried much of the passenger traffic across the Firth to Burntisland in Fife. With the construction of Granton Harbour, most of this traffic was lost.

The EP&D management had by no means been blind to the problem, for four transhipments of goods necessary between Granton and Broughty Ferry were vastly wasteful of time, expense and in fact were a constant source of damage and pilfering. Long before Bouch's arrival the Directors had consulted Thomas Grainger. His solution, which turned out to be little more than a makeshift, was to fit the ferries with rails laid on the decks, and to use hydraulic cranes on the dockside to lift wagons on and off. This proposal was accepted by the Directors, and a number of hydraulic cranes, patented in 1846 and possibly the first in the world, were ordered from W.G. Armstrong, Manager of the famous engineering works at Elswick-on-Tyne. This method of working proved unacceptably slow – it took some five minutes to transfer each wagon to or from the ferry.

Bouch turned his mind to a quicker mode of transferring wagons, and with the help of his able assistant, William Hall, to whom much of the credit for the success of the scheme is due, Bouch proposed a moving cradle. This would move up and down an inclined ramp at each harbour to accommodate changes in tidal levels. The cradle carried two lines of rails which at the lower end would line up with the rails on the decks of the ferries. By this means wagons could be handled expeditiously in batches instead of singly, on what Bouch called the 'flying bridge'. The system was not infallible. On rare occasions wagons would fail to stop and career over the bows into the harbour one by one, but it was incomparably superior to what had gone before.

The original steamers were small and a constant source of trouble. Their crews knew little of their duties, and since sea water was used in the boilers, they demanded constant attention and frequent replacement. Granton Harbour was well supplied with fresh water although there was little in the immediate vicinity, for the Duke had carried a pipeline from springs on Corstorphine Hill, several miles away to the south. This supplied all the hydraulic cranes, which were fed from a high-level tank, with the hydraulic pressure provided by a steam pumping engine. The purchase of two much larger ferries, designed by Thomas Grainger, had been approved prior to Bouch's appointment, the order going to Robert Napier & Sons, the well-known Clyde shipbuilders. The slightly larger one for the Forth crossing was appropriately named *Leviathan*. The Tay crossing was much shorter and a smaller ferry was sufficient.

The new ferries were specified by Grainger to be double-ended, with three lines of rails running the length of a flat deck. On *Leviathan* the deck was 167ft long and 35ft between the paddle boxes, and could accommodate thirty-four wagons. The vessel was registered at Granton as being of 299 gross tons with a draft of 8½ft. Each paddle had its own engine of 210hp with a pair of 56in x 42in cylinders, one engine with its own boiler on either side of the hull, and since the paddles could be worked independently the ship was very manoeuvrable. It was 1 March 1850 before *Leviathan* entered service, and the 'flying bridges' operated impeccably. Still only twenty-eight years of age, Bouch's reputation spread rapidly, but he realised that if he was to get on in the world he needed greater opportunities than the EP&D could offer. He had greatly enhanced the business of the company, but now had come the time to move on. He was unintentionally given a helping hand by the little St Andrews Railway, which became his first commission.

The First of the Economical Railways

It is more than likely that others before Bouch had realised that, if the rural areas were to receive an affordable rail service, then something more economical would be needed than the magnificent main lines such as Grainger & Miller's E&G, or Locke & Errington's trunk line from Carlisle to Glasgow and Aberdeen. One exception was the NBR between Edinburgh and Berwick which was poorly engineered but cost just as much. The Royal Burgh of Haddington was bypassed for economic reasons, but then had to be given its own double-line branch and a station to match. Ten years later, due to lack of traffic, the line was singled.

In the middle of the nineteenth century, after the euphoria of the Railway Mania had subsided, there were thousands of unfortunate, and in many cases foolhardy, investors who were left to lick their financial wounds and swear that never again would they dabble in railway shares. The result was that for several years there was a great shortage of capital for railway development. Although it had proved possible to build Scottish main lines more economically than in England, this was attributable in large part to lower land prices and fewer built-up areas, with the result that in Scotland costs per mile were only on average 84% of those further south. To offset this advantage Scottish traffic receipts were lower, and operating expenses swallowed 53% of the revenue as against 46% in England. North or south, engineers' fees were in the region of £500 per mile of line.

It was widely recognised that in rural areas the cost of railway building had to be cut to the bone if they were ever to receive an essential service. To the agricultural industry dealing in bulk materials of limited unit value like potatoes, or requiring coal, lime and fertiliser, the availability of rail transport led to expanded markets, and savings which could be invested in buildings and land improvements. Few engineers or landowners were prepared to invest until they saw how others profited.

The St Andrews Railway

Bouch, however, was given an early opportunity to put his ideas into practice, and the St Andrews Railway was the first where he could practise 'strict economy'. By cutting his own fees to £100 a mile instead of the £500 a mile demanded by other engineers he no doubt became unpopular among his peers. Nevertheless, this allowed lines to be built, and even run profitably, which otherwise would never have seen the light of day. Some eventually developed out of all proportion to their humble beginnings as traffic increased over the years, and in the course of time they were reconstructed to higher standards to handle the increased traffic.

This branch ran from the EP&D at Milton near Leuchars to the ancient university town of St Andrews on the coast 4½ miles to the east. Though the line was projected locally, it was from the beginning taken under the wing of the EP&D which supplied the engineering expertise in the person of Bouch. It was agreed that the EP&D would duly work the line on completion. The branch had been suggested as early as 1845, but it was not until a public meeting on 19 December 1850, chaired by the Provost of St Andrews, that things came to a head. Bouch, who would shortly take over as a freelance consultant, prepared the Parliamentary survey and a Bill was presented to Parliament early in the 1851 Session. The Act was granted on 3 July 1851 and work started early in September. It may be assumed that Bouch had discussed the situation with the EP&D, because when he offered his resignation in March 1851 he was allowed to continue to supervise the St Andrews line in his private capacity. His fees of £100 per mile must have been an attraction, and this contract allowed Bouch to hit the ground running as an independent consulting engineer.

From his first arrival in Scotland Bouch had given much thought to the future development of railways in rural areas north of the border. While this seemed to be a matter of common sense, Bouch was the first to put the principle into practice. A number of trunk lines had already been completed at the then average going rate of £32,000 per mile, whereas in England the rate was £6,000 higher, with the greater cost of land being the most likely cause of the difference, English landowners became notoriously rapacious at the sight of a railway surveyor. If branch lines were to serve the smaller communities, economies had to be made somewhere. This was best achieved by limiting civil engineering works to a minimum, coupled with the use of light locomotives, rolling stock and permanent way. Bouch's estimate for the St Andrews branch was under £5,000 a mile. The day of the light railway had arrived, although this title would not receive official recognition until the Railway Regulation Act of 1868.

Apart from foregoing £1,800 of his professional fees, Bouch exercised strict economy in all respects of the construction. The rails were of 60lbs/yd section, obtained second-hand from the EP&D, but the sleepers were spaced 4ft apart instead of the customary three, and the light cast-iron chairs were secured to the sleepers with wooden trenails (hardwood pegs) instead of spikes. Within months of opening, the defects in the permanent way became obvious, and following a derailment in 1856 when, as a result of increasing traffic, an attempt was made to run a heavier locomotive, these weaknesses could no longer be ignored and had to be remedied at much expense, bringing the costs up to £5,600 per mile. Still a very reasonable figure. In spite of the availability of 'Kyanising' and other wood treatments, the two timber viaducts over the Eden and Motram Water, as well as the sleepers, were constructed of untreated timber and enjoyed short lives in consequence. A false economy to some, though a saving of money in Bouch's book, which he repeated elsewhere. As late as 1864, after two years in the ownership of the NBR, much still remained to be done. Following a minor derailment the Inspecting Officer reported:

> The line itself is of very light and poor construction. The rails are single headed in lengths of 16ft and are considerably worn. [They were life-expired main line rails from the NBR.] Joint and intermediate chairs are weak, too narrow in the throat to admit a good key, and reported to be continually breaking. (NOTE: No fishplates were used, the joints being accommodated in extra wide chairs.)

Within its limitations, mostly arising from Bouch's passion for economy, the St Andrews Railway was a modest success, but the EP&D was heavily criticised for the poor accommodation and bad train connections which it provided at the junction station at Leuchars, and this was a matter not under Bouch's control. Even two years after the NBR had taken over in 1862 the *Dundee Courier* reported that:

> A more ill-provided junction does not exist on the line. The waiting room for First and Second Class passengers is a small circumscribed compartment or rather box, with three wooden chairs and a small fire, minus a poker, in a grate scarcely fit for a ploughman's bothy. What we have said of the compartment for gentlemen applies equally for the room for ladies. Both rooms are simply despicable. The fact is that the station was never meant for a junction at all, being originally built for the village of Leuchars alone, and no additional accommodation has been provided after the construction of the St Andrews branch.

It would appear that when the junction was formed at Milton, to save expense the original Leuchars building had been uprooted and moved down the line.

3

MARRIAGE, FAMILY
AND A NEW HOUSE

In 1848, as a first step on the professional ladder, Bouch had been granted the Diploma of the Royal Scottish Society of Arts. To the Victorians there was no clear distinction between the fine arts and the useful arts. Beyond doubt engineering was a useful art and Bouch became a respected member of the Society. Anxious to further improve his standing in his chosen profession, he then applied for Associate Membership of the Institution of Civil Engineers, writing from the EP&D Railway office. On 5 November 1850 his application was approved by Council and balloted for on 3 December. His Proposer was his old master Joseph Locke. His referees included such well-known names as William Henry Barlow, John Hawkshaw, John Errington and Charles Hutton Gregory.

In 1858 Bouch went on to apply for full membership of the Institution and this was passed by Council on 11 May. In promoting his own interests Bouch was not one to do things by halves, and once again his Proposer was Joseph Locke, now one of the most eminent civil engineers of the day. Bouch had earned himself a good reputation when working as an apprentice surveyor under George Larmer on Locke's Lancaster & Carlisle Railway and this had not been forgotten. Not content with this, Bouch had rounded up a formidable list of Seconders including Locke's partner, John Errington, John Fowler, George Parker Bidder, Charles Hutton Gregory, William Henry Barlow, John Hawkshaw, and his old employer at Leeds, George Leather. With such eminent support his application could hardly fail nor did it. One unexplained mystery is why Bouch gave his address as North St David Street, a short street leading from St Andrew's Square to Queen Street. He is reported to have had his first office there and may have retained it.

Bouch had by then settled into a small office at 1 Hanover Street, just off Princes Street, in 1851, but quickly finding himself short of space he moved in 1853 to larger premises at 78 George Street where he remained for many years. Some time early in 1853 he had taken an apartment at 31 Nelson Street, one of the less-fashionable streets of the New Town but suited to his still modest means. Bouch's name does not appear at that address in the 1851 census, but among the four occupants of the flats was Agnes Renwick, lodging housekeeper, from whom he might have been renting. The other occupants were Mary Fraser whose husband was in the service of the East India Co., James Hastie, tea, wine and spirit merchant, and Christian Rymer, annuitant.

A recent view of Sir Thomas Bouch's house at 6 Oxford Terrace, off the Queensferry Road in Edinburgh. No. 6 is the slightly larger house in the middle of the terrace. Although now divided into flats, the external appearance remains much as Bouch must have known it a century and a half ago.

Courting in Coatbridge

Whenever a chance arose Bouch put on his best suit, gave an extra polish to his boots, and took the train to Coatbridge, just outside Glasgow, where he successfully courted Margaret Terrie Nelson, a young lady of twenty-one years of age at the time of her marriage in 1853. Her father, Thomas Nelson, was a member of the well-known Nelson family of railway contractors, which also had associations with Carlisle, where they may have first met. Thomas Nelson worked mainly in the North of England, but occasionally ventured over the Scottish border in later years when his son had joined him in the business.

In 1855 their first daughter, Fanny, was born, followed two years later by Elizabeth Ann. The flat at 31 Nelson Street was becoming too small for a growing family, and he and Margaret were still hoping for a son to follow his father into the engineering profession. By now the financial situation was much easier, with Bouch's reputation becoming more widely known, and he was receiving an abundance of new commissions. Then as now, property in the New Town commanded a premium price, and a new development over the Dean Bridge and along the Queensferry Road, on the high western bank of the Water of Leith, looked promising. The land formed part of the Dean Estate which was owned by John Learmonth, promoter and first Chairman of the NBR. In 1832, to encourage building on the Dean Estate, Learmonth, by then Lord Provost of Edinburgh, had commissioned Thomas Telford to build the Dean Bridge over the Water of Leith, which solved the problem of access from the New Town. Oxford Terrace formed part of an upmarket development aimed at the professional classes, with a number of houses having mews cottages for their coachmen. Although No.6 Oxford Terrace had a fair-sized garden and a rear entrance off Lennox Street Lane, there was no accommodation for a coachman, and Bouch probably rented one of the mews in Lennox Street Lane. His office in George Street was only about a mile and a half distant, and a pleasant walk on a fine day. Later, for his more distant journeys over the NBR system, a private carriage was provided by the company which could be attached to any convenient train when needed.

John Learmonth was already Chairman of the Edinburgh & Glasgow Railway when he first promoted the idea of a railway east of Edinburgh to Dunbar, and in due course to Berwick where a link could be made with the English railway system. Learmonth was destined to become a powerful figure in Scottish business circles. His efforts to promote the North British Railway were hampered by lack of capital in Scotland, or at least the lack of the will to risk it on railways, and in desperation likely investors were approached in an attempt to sell shares from door to door. It was not until Learmonth had made strenuous efforts south of the border to promote the Berwick to Edinburgh line that things started to look up, and despite a dispute with the all-powerful George Hudson, the money was eventually forthcoming and the company incorporated on 4 July 1844. The Commissioners of Woods and Forests had to be placated by offering to enclose the line where it passed close to Holyrood House lest Her Majesty's repose should be disturbed.

A broad explanation of the Scottish system of land tenure may be helpful before discussing Bouch's new house at 6 Oxford Terrace. While in theory the freehold of all Scottish land was vested in the Crown, over the centuries land was acquired by various means and the Crown 'tenants' became known as the Feu Superiors. If one of these Superiors such as John Learmonth wished to develop part of his estate, he could feu (lease) it to, say, a developer, in return for a payment and a feu duty (or ground rent) payable in perpetuity. This would be subject to strict conditions, listed in the Feu Charter, as to the form of the development and the number, size and general character of any buildings to be erected on the feu. Feus could be subdivided, allowing each house within a development to be sold off, subject to the approval of the Superior at all stages. Within the burghs, building controls affecting structural matters and general health and safety were enforced by the Dean of Guild Courts. Since 1874 major changes have amended feudal law and this is a rough account of how the law stood in the 1850s. Bouch received a typical feu charter:

> Feu Charter by the Trustees of the late John Learmonth to Thomas Bouch. At Edinburgh on the 16th day of May, One thousand eight hundred and fifty nine.

Like an English lease, strict conditions were laid down as to how the ground should be used, no obnoxious trades such as a brewery or a skinworks and so on, to preserve the amenity of the neighbourhood, no extensions without the permission of the Feu Superior, and of course an annual feu duty must be paid without fail.

In this case the late John Learmonth would appear to have undertaken the development himself, and the dwelling house and land were 'disponed' to Thomas Bouch for the sum of £1,920 Sterling. Added to this there were the costs of decorating and furnishing such a large house and, all in all, he must have spent around £3,000, of which £2,000 is said to have been borrowed on a mortgage. The financial problems of a decade earlier following the Railway Mania were all but forgotten, work was now plentiful, and by this time Bouch could well afford the outlay.

Today, 6 Oxford Terrace remains externally much as Bouch must have known it, though now it is subdivided into flats. The iron railings at the front survived the wartime vandalism when so many of Edinburgh's railings were removed for scrap and then dumped in the sea as useless. At the garden level was the kitchen and the usual domestic offices, and on the ground floor may have been two 'public rooms' and a study. To the front on the first floor three tall windows, with a handsome cast-iron balcony outside, gave light to the drawing room, with the master bedroom and a dressing room to the rear. On the second floor were the nursery and the bedrooms for the children, and in the attics above slept the servants. Speculation perhaps, but this would have been typical for a house of the period.

By the time of the 1861 Census the household had grown and there were three servants, including a nursemaid to look after the three children. Bouch's hopes had been realised in 1859 when Margaret had presented him with a son, named William after his uncle and grandfather.

Once settled into their new house, family life for the Bouch's seems to have been generally uneventful. While the iniquities of the servant classes always provided a talking point in drawing rooms and around dinner tables, the fact that there were good servants and bad employers was not widely discussed except 'below stairs'. A rapid turnover of servants marked out the unsatisfactory employers. Thomas and Margaret Bouch must have exercised a benign rule, for of the three female servants recorded in 1861 two were still there ten years later, though by then there was little call for the services of a nursery maid. In 1861 Isabella (twenty-nine) and Margaret Heggie (twenty) and Mary Bain (twenty) from Whitekirk in East Lothian had joined the household, and by 1871 Isabella Heggie had moved on, and had probably married, while Margaret Gordon (twenty-eight) of Gladsmuir, East Lothian, had taken over Isabella Heggie's job as cook. Margaret Heggie was still listed as nurse.

How the children were educated is not recorded. Probably a visiting governess sufficed while they were young, and peripatetic teachers of ladylike accomplishments would teach needlework, painting, music and dancing to the girls. For William there was Daniel Stewart's College for Boys which had opened in 1855 about half a mile to the west on the Queensferry Road. William's formal education finished when he was fifteen and he became an indentured pupil in his father's office, with the Deed of Apprenticeship, which had been drawn-up by the family lawyer, kept securely in his father's desk. Bouch had long dreamed of this auspicious day. This may not have been entirely William's personal choice of occupation, for the start of his professional career, first on the Tay Bridge and then on the Arbroath & Montrose Railway, was unpromising to say the least, and after his father's death he used his very considerable inheritance to live the life of a country squire at Ashorne House in Warwickshire.

There is no doubt that religion played an important part in the life of the Bouchs, just as it did in the lives of virtually every middle-class family in Victorian times. To attend church on a Sunday was a conventional social act and did not necessarily imply deep religious convictions. It was the done thing and nowhere more so than in Scotland under the influence of the Presbyterian Church and its offshoots. The North British Railway was one of the very few to run Sunday trains because of the influence of its majority of English shareholders who cared more for Mammon than Scottish sensibilities.

Thomas Bouch had been brought up in the bosom of the Church of England at Thursby, and when he moved to Scotland he naturally turned to the Episcopal Church, which even today is sometimes referred to as the 'English Church'. The Episcopalians were forever at odds with the Presbyterians though doctrinally they had much in common and had sprung from common roots. The differences were mainly political or concerned matters of Church governance. The Episcopalians appointed Bishops, which was anathema to the established Church of Scotland where one critic denounced Bishops as 'the caterpillars of the Church'. The Episcopalians tended to have a more liberal outlook, and this attracted the upper classes who resented the powers of the Kirk Session to call them publicly to account.

Holy Trinity Episcopal Church at the Dean Bridge was opened in 1838 and was conveniently situated for families from Oxford Terrace. While it was further from Nelson Street, Bouch may have attended there from his arrival in Edinburgh, since until the mid-century Episcopal Churches were thin on the ground. It was from Holy Trinity that in 1880 Bouch's impressive funeral cortege would set out for his final resting place in the Dean Cemetery, which had been developed on part of Learmonth's estate in 1845.

Apart from occasional bills and references to his growing art collection, little documentary evidence relating to everyday life at 6 Oxford Terrace has survived. Bouch's unmarried sister, Elizabeth Ann (more generally known as Ann), stayed on at Thursby until her death at the age of eighty-four. Margaret seems to have taken no direct part in Bouch's business affairs. She was content to look after the children and to keep the household running smoothly. As his business prospered Bouch was away on his various projects in the North of England, and as far afield as London and Kent. Apart from three months abroad in the interests of his health, when the strain of the Tay Bridge was beginning to tell, Bouch seems never to have gone to any foreign countries, and even at home took no part in Edinburgh high society. He was more at home in the Royal Scottish Society of Arts, where in 1877 he was elected a Member of Council, than in the more rarefied circles of the Royal Society of Edinburgh. His friends were fellow engineers and several of the NBR Directors, as well as architects, and other practical men like Robert Bow and Allan Duncan Stewart.

At this point it would be appropriate to describe the numerous small railways with which Bouch was involved over the next twenty years. The more important works will be dealt with at greater length in other chapters. Rather than attempt to deal with them chronologically, they will be grouped geographically from north to south.

However, there was one railway which drew Bouch back to Coatbridge, known as the Glasgow & Coatbridge Railway, with its terminus at College, otherwise known as High Street. This offered an alternative route from Edinburgh should the main line be closed, but its long-term importance was eventually to allow an attack on the Caledonian monopoly in the west of Scotland. The Edinburgh end of the line started as a branch from the Edinburgh & Glasgow main line at Ratho to the West Lothian town of Bathgate and opened on 12 November 1849. An extension, the Bathgate & Coatbridge Railway, opened on 11 August 1862. Finally the Glasgow & Coatbridge, with Bouch as engineer, was opened on 1 April 1871. As a diversionary route it did not allow high speeds as a result of curves and gradients, but it passed through an extensive mineral district, where coal, ironstone and oil shale were extensively worked.

Between Coatbridge and Glasgow there were few heavy engineering works, except an iron lattice girder viaduct at Bargeddie where the manufacturer had ignored the specification and placed his rivets at 4in centres instead of the required 3ins. This could seriously affect the strength of the girders. There was also a masonry viaduct at Drumpellier which caused some concern, though details are lacking. In 1865 the North British acquired control of the Clyde Coast line as far as Helensburgh, and in 1886 the link between College and Queen Street, low level to Clydebank, allowed a through NBR service from Edinburgh to Helensburgh. From there in 1894 the line was extended to Fort William, and on 1 April 1901 the ferry and fishing port of Mallaig was reached. In 1960 electrification of lines north of the Clyde was started, and electric services continue to run over Bouch's Glasgow & Coatbridge Railway to Coatbridge and Airdrie. There are now serious proposals to reopen the line between Airdrie and Bathgate for passenger traffic, once again allowing an alternative route for through trains between Edinburgh and Glasgow, some fifty years after the previous service had been withdrawn in January 1956. Freight services between Bathgate and Airdrie lasted until 1982. This route had opened in 1862, but there is no record of Bouch being involved east of Coatbridge.

4

THOMAS BOUCH, SURVEYOR:
RAILWAYS, HORSE TRAMS AND A PIER

With his training on the Lancaster & Carlisle Railway, Bouch was better qualified than most to undertake railway survey work. Plans for some of the lines did not mature, whilst others were completed at a later date by other engineers. Many have gone unrecorded.

The NBR had opened what it referred to as the Hawick Branch on 20 February 1849, and there for the time being it stopped. Initially this branch was a white elephant and lost money, and many shareholders were far from happy. However, a continuation through to Carlisle promised a cure for this and would be undertaken in due time. Competition for this route was between the NBR and the Caledonian, and it was a hard-fought battle. Although the Caledonian already possessed an entirely adequate main line north from Carlisle, its main aim was to prevent further expansion south by the NBR, and it did not envisage through traffic to Edinburgh. Richard Hodgson, Chairman of the NBR, was aiming for a first-class main line which would connect Edinburgh to Carlisle and all points south. This, he hoped, would attract much traffic away from the Caledonian.

In June 1857 Hodgson wrote to the Caledonian management, suggesting a meeting of the various interested companies to try and reach a compromise. He heard nothing until September, when a meeting was agreed between Hodgson and Lt-Col Salkeld, Deputy Chairman of the Caledonian, and two interested landowners. No agreement was reached, and the following year the Caledonian submitted their Carlisle & Hawick Bill. To Hodgson's relief and that of the NBR, the Caledonian Bill was rejected by the House of Lords. It was in the survey for that line that Bouch became involved when he assisted Benjamin Hall Blyth, three years his senior but welcoming Bouch's surveying experience.

Blyth worked extensively for the Caledonian on new work, and had served his pupilage in the office of Grainger and Miller, where he stayed until 1850 when he set up as a consulting engineer with an office in Edinburgh. In 1854 he took his brother Edward into partnership. He died in 1866 but the firm in one form or another has survived until today and the name of Blyth & Blyth is well known in Edinburgh engineering circles.

Since this was purely a blocking action by the Caledonian, which had no ambitions to run beyond Hawick, although an extension to Galashiels had been contemplated, a single line was thought to be adequate, but it received little local support, for Hawick was looking for a main line outlet to the south and not some little branch line. In the next Parliamentary Session in 1859 the NBR put forward its Border Union Bill for a steeply graded line rising to a summit at Whitrope, then falling steadily to Newcastleton and downhill virtually all the way to Carlisle. The Caledonian plans had blocked the much easier route through Langholm, and there remained the danger that they might be revived. To a certain extent the Caledonian had achieved its dog-in-the-manger purpose, though there was much rejoicing in the towns and villages like Newcastleton on the more populous route chosen by the NBR, leaving only the small mill town of Langholm languishing at the end of a branch.

The Wigtownshire Railway

For many years there were no railways west of Dumfries, which was first served by the Glasgow & South Western Railway in 1850. It was not until six years later that firm proposals were made for a line to reach Stranraer and Portpatrick, passing through the county town of Wigtown, which had a population in the region of 2,000. B. & E. Blyth, consulting engineers of 135 George Street, Edinburgh, were instructed to carry out the survey for a Bill to be put before Parliament in the 1857 Session. Because the scheme was not well supported locally, the company, like the NBR at its birth, was reduced to selling shares from door to door. The Act was passed in 1858, and the last contract was let early in 1859. Opening of the line took place in two stages, from Dumfries to Castle Douglas on 7 November 1859, and Castle Douglas to Stranraer on 12 March 1861.

The hopes of the burghers of Wigtown had been dashed when the line was built several miles to the east via Creetown, and in 1863 a public meeting was called to propose the construction of a line from Newton Stewart to the coast at Whithorn, passing through Wigtown. This would serve some of the best agricultural land in the county. It was also hoped that the Irish trade through the harbour at Whithorn could be increased. Thomas Bouch was instructed to carry out a full survey with a view to preparing a Bill. Nothing came of this, but another scheme, closely following Bouch's survey, was put forward when the matter was revived in September 1871, though it took until July 1877 before the line reached Whithorn. The engineers were again the Blyth & Blyth partnership, though Benjamin Blyth himself had died of overwork on 21 August 1866 at the early age of forty-seven.

The Lancashire Union Railway

Railways in Lancashire tended broadly to run north and south, and there was a call for an east and west line to link these so that coal from the Wigan collieries could more easily reach the cotton manufacturing towns in the east of the county. Elias Dorning was a young civil engineer from Manchester who, at the early age of twenty-four, set up in business as a civil and mining engineer, surveyor and land agent, though his experience of railway work was limited. Nonetheless, he was employed by the LNWR to make a survey and acquire land for a line between Eccles, Tyldesley, Wigan and Leigh, which had already received its Act on 11 July 1861. Bouch was three years younger but more experienced in railway work, and it was probably for this reason that Dorning invited him to become joint engineer. By then Bouch's work for the S&D would have become well known in the North of England.

Railways in the area were complicated by the existence of three other companies besides the LUR. The North Union Railway (later part of the LNWR), the Lancashire & Yorkshire Railway and the Great Central all had a web of lines, and for good measure the LNWR and the L&YR operated several joint lines. Dorning and Bouch remained engineers for the LUR, with George Lee as resident engineer. There were four bridges which were probably attributable to Bouch on the scanty evidence that three used the X diagonal bracing which was his trademark.

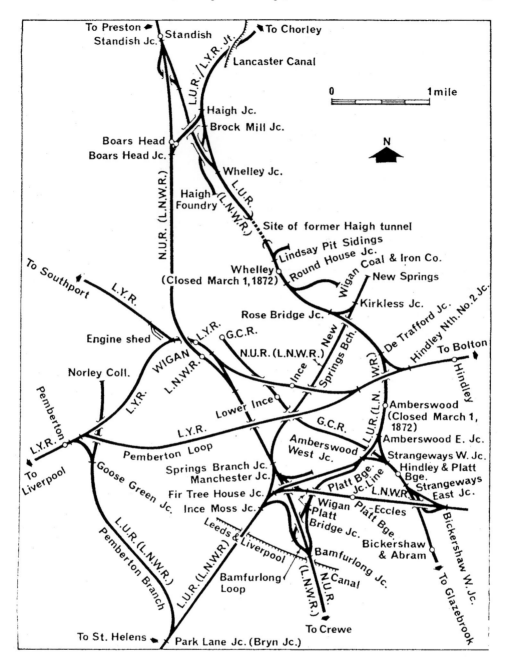

Network of railways in the Wigan area in 1900.

Aqueduct carrying Lancaster Canal.

Botany Row Viaduct, April 1968.

Carr Mill Viaduct, April 1969.

Viaduct over the river Douglas, April 1969.

Just north of St Helen's was the Carr Mill Viaduct, with six spans of 40ft on brick piers. Between Boars Head and Haigh Junctions, where the LUR crossed the valley of the river Douglas, there was an iron viaduct with seven 55ft spans on brick piers, standing 86ft above the valley.

These girders for the Douglas Viaduct were of the inverted braced bowstring type, much the same as Bouch had used on the Cockermouth, Keswick & Penrith and still somewhat unusual at that date. Further on towards Chorley an aqueduct was provided to carry the Lancaster Canal over the LUR on a skew span of about 60ft. The canal was carried in a brick channel supported by iron lattice girders. The only major masonry viaduct was nearer to Chorley at Botany Brow, and here the LUR was carried over the valley and the Lancaster Canal on nine spans of 33ft at a height of 48ft.

The Swanley, Seven Oaks (sic) and Maidstone Railway

This started as a small rural line running from a new junction on the London, Chatham & Dover Railway near Swanley and terminating at Sevenoaks (Bat and Ball), named after an adjacent public house. Up to that time the South Eastern had hoped to enjoy a monopoly of the fast-growing traffic to London from their station at Sevenoaks (Tubs Hill). It is not clear how Bouch became involved in a project so far south, but perhaps his reputation for economical railway building had preceded him. The line to Sevenoaks was authorised on 1 August 1859 and completed on 2 June 1862. The same year approval was given for the branch to Maidstone (East) with a junction at Otford. This did not open until 1 June 1874.

Engineering works were fairly heavy between Swanley and Otford, with gradients up to 1:101 for considerable distances, and due to the hilly nature of the country there was a tunnel 820 yards in length, and at Eynsford it was necessary to build a masonry viaduct, having nine arches of 30ft span, over the valley of the Darent. This was followed by a cutting of about a mile in length and up to 70ft deep before reaching Otford.

In this case, being so far from home, Bouch probably did the survey and Parliamentary work, but the construction was left to an experienced resident engineer. One feature which definitely showed the hand of Bouch was the bridge over the Medway at Maidstone. This was of the bowstring type, but not the heavy design he had used elsewhere. It did closely resemble the two bowstring girders of remarkably light appearance used at the northern end of the Tay Bridge, which were the work of Allan Stewart. Later the line was extended through to Ashford, offering an alternative route to Dover.

As the years passed the whole area developed rapidly, and it was necessarily shortly after completion to double both lines. The next major change came with electrification by the Southern Railway in January 1935. Probably what would have astounded Bouch most was that the line has been upgraded as an alternative route for trains from Waterloo to the Channel Tunnel. This is one of the few of his lines that has survived into the twenty-first century.

Street Tramways and a Seaside Pier

By the end of the 1860s railways were well developed and most of the national network had already been constructed, therefore it is perhaps surprising that the use of railed transport on public roads had been delayed so long. While the first London omnibus ran on 4 July 1829, promoted by the pioneering George Shillibeer, it would be another thirty-two years before an American, George Francis Train, was permitted to build an experimental tram line along a part of Bayswater Road from Marble Arch to Porchester Terrace. This opened on 23 March 1861. Two other short lines quickly followed.

This substantial nine-arch viaduct by Thomas Bouch, which crosses the Darent Valley, lies between Swanley and Otford on the line to Sevenoaks and Maidstone. Today it provides an alternative route for the Eurostar between Swanley and Ashford.

The single-deck car, drawn by two horses, was of quite a sophisticated design based on thirty years' development in America. Unfortunately, such was the degree of public criticism that within a few months all three lines were gone and Train with them.

Train made two fundamental errors. He laid his lines in middle-class districts where those who did not possess their own carriages could well afford cabs, and as a result there was a limited demand for public transport. Moreover, he insisted upon using edge rails which rose above the road surface by about ¾in, causing an obstruction and danger to horse traffic. Neither was Train's bombastic 'Yankee' persona well received, and there was growing competition from the surface railways which were pressing ahead with their suburban networks, while the below ground Metropolitan Railway was already under construction. Train's failure set back the development of street tramways by almost a decade, and Liverpool, which received its Act of Parliament in 1868, was the first major British city to adopt the street tramway successfully. However, Portsmouth was the first

The unusually light high level bridge by Bouch over the Medway at Maidstone, with a span of 113ft. His only other bridge of similar design was at the north end of the Tay Bridge with a span of 160ft. The Maidstone bridge was replaced in 1927.

to have a street tramway authorised by Act of Parliament as early as 8 June 1863. It was opened on 15 May 1865 but was just over a mile in length.

London's first purpose-built underground railway was the Metropolitan, opened on 9 January 1863, running mostly under what was then known as the New Road, from Farringdon Street in the City to Paddington, where there was a link to the GWR at Bishop's Road. Mixed-gauge track allowed broad-gauge trains to run through to Farringdon Street. The engineer was John Fowler, whose firm of consulting engineers was on its way to becoming the largest in the country. The railway was built by the cut-and-cover system and there was no deep tunnelling. Since the tunnels were only a few feet underground ventilation was not a great problem, and special condensing steam locomotives were built known as 'Fowler's ghosts' because they ran so quietly. Dark and smoky the new-fangled underground railway may have been, but it was chosen by many in preference to the discomforts of the horse buses. Extensions quickly followed. Parliament, concerned at the prospects of a London version of the Railway Mania, set up a Select Committee to advise on the shape of future developments, including a possible 'inner circuit' to extend the existing Metropolitan through Kensington and Westminster, and along the north bank of the Thames to the City. Engineers were invited to submit proposals, and among others both Fowler and Bouch prepared schemes. It was Fowler's plan that was approved in principle.

Thomas Bouch was always alert to new developments, and he kept a small office in Westminster to act as a base for his work in attending Parliamentary Committees, and for drumming up new business. The office was run for a time by Mr John Wood, an experienced railway engineer, and later by Mr Peddie from the Edinburgh office. Bouch's function was to prepare the Parliamentary surveys, for tramways, like railways, needed an individual Private Act of Parliament to be passed. He would then nurse the Bill through the Committee stages when technical questions were raised. In the case of tramways he does not appear to have become involved with the actual construction and operation, though he did take shares in one London company. Despite having this Westminster office Bouch does not seem to have been accepted as 'one of us' by his London colleagues, and only rarely did he attend meetings of the Institution of Civil Engineers. Being regarded as a provincial and something of a maverick, he was not always treated with the respect he felt that he deserved, especially by some of the younger members.

With two notable exceptions, to be described later, Bouch confined himself to railway works, and he considered himself to be particularly well fitted to survey street tramways when they first sprang into prominence in the late 1860s. After Liverpool had shown the way in 1868, it was the following year when three schemes were approved in London. North of the Thames ran the North Metropolitan Tramways. South of the river the Metropolitan Street Tramways were approved. Both were engineered by George Hopkins who was also in charge of the Liverpool venture. The third London company was the Pimlico, Peckham & Greenwich, where Thomas Bouch was engineer and a substantial shareholder, holding about 1/6 of the issued capital. By 1871 the line was open through from Greenwich to the south side of Westminster Bridge, and by 1874 the Company operated nearly 25 miles of track and a stock of over 330 horse cars. Bouch found he had made a sound investment.

Scotland's first horse tramway was built by the Edinburgh Street Tramways Co., which received its Act in 1871, and the first cars started running on 6 November the same year. The first line ran from the West End and along Princes Street to the General Post Office, thence down Leith Walk to Bernard Street, Leith, and in 1872 the line was extended over the North Bridge to Newington. Bouch was the man on the spot, and could boast of his experience in London. He was commissioned to plan the layout and attend to all the Parliamentary work, but the construction and operation was the responsibility of the Company's own engineer, John Macrae. Plans were drawn up for a pair of semi-detached houses in Primrose Bank, Trinity (as it then was), to house the Manager and the engineer, but these were never built and the site lay vacant until the present houses were built in 1895-6. The local belief that Bouch had a hand in their building is clearly without foundation.

Although Glasgow had received their Street Tramways Act in 1870, well ahead of their Edinburgh rivals, for some reason work was slow progressing, and the opening was delayed until 19 August 1872. The first route was quite short, from St George's Cross and through the city centre to Eglinton Toll, on the south bank of the Clyde. Eventually it would grow into a system of over 140 route miles. An uncommon feature was that the tracks were laid to a gauge of 4ft 7¾ins to allow standard railway wagons to be run over parts of the tramway system to serve various industrial premises. This was not unique. For instance, tramways in the Portsmouth area adopted the same gauge for the same reason. This was another venture for which Bouch did all the preliminary work, but was not involved in the construction. Bouch's only other tramway work in Scotland was for the tiny Dundee system. Although this received its Act in 1872 it was only on 30 August 1877 that the first 1¼-mile section was opened. At its peak as a horse-drawn system it was less than 6 route miles in length.

It may reasonably be claimed that Bouch made a substantial contribution to street tramways in their most formative years.

The Pier at Portobello

Mention was made earlier of Bouch's involvement in a matter totally unconnected with railways. One was the road bridge at Redheugh, Newcastle upon Tyne, which will be described in Chapter 8. The second was the seaside pier at Portobello, then a small town

Above, below and opposite: The long-forgotten pier at Portobello, designed by Thomas Bouch. As a result of a shortage of funds, on completion Bouch took it over and he and his wife ran it successfully for many years. On his death it was sold to the proprietor of a fleet of pleasure steamers operating on the Forth.

north of the city on the shores of the Firth of Forth, and in Victorian times it became a popular watering place. Not only did Bouch design and build the pier, but he and his family ran it successfully for a number of years. The shoreline at Portobello is very exposed to storms, and two previous attempts to build a promenade had been washed away.

In earlier days the area was a sandy scrub-covered wilderness, inhabited only by thieves, vagabonds and robbers. However, the old Musselburgh Road reached the shore near the mouth of the Figgate Burn, and there a small harbour sheltered a few fishing boats. Towards the end of the eighteenth century the village started to grow, and by 1810 boasted a parish church. As the town grew so too did the number of places of worship, and by 1876 there were eight in use. The manufacture of bricks, tiles and bottles provided employment. As early as 1806 a suite of hot and cold seawater baths had been provided to cater for the many summer visitors from Edinburgh and further afield. The arrival of the railway in 1846 and horse trams from Edinburgh in May 1875 greatly increased the number of day trippers. It was clear to the Provost and Town Council of Portobello that a pier was needed to keep up with other high-class watering places, and in 1868 Bouch was commissioned to prepare a suitable design. His first estimate for construction was £7,000.

Before any work on a pier could start the seawall had to be completed. The first wall built in 1866 was swept away by the spring tides of 1867, and its successor was similarly destroyed ten years later. The old harbour had been allowed to silt up until it became no better than a cesspool. Visitors wishing to enjoy boat trips had to wade out to the boats or be carried out on the backs of the boatmen. In 1868 the Portobello Pier Co. was set up with the encouragement of Provost Wood and with Bouch as engineer. The capital was to be raised by issuing 700 shares of £10 each. The local inhabitants showed little interest, since a similar scheme a few years before to build a Town Hall had fallen by the wayside with considerable losses. Eventually Bouch and members of his family agreed to put up the bulk of the capital. In March 1869 the Bill went before both Houses of Parliament, but caused a great uproar in Portobello because it was discovered, rather late in the day, that it contained no provision against opening on the Sabbath. The Bill passed the House of Lords without this vital condition, and Provost Wood was sent off to London post-haste to see if the Bill could be altered in the Commons. After much negotiation it was amended and passed on 10 June 1869. It then had to return to the Lords, and Lord Redesdale resolutely opposed any mention of closure on Sundays. As he remarked to Provost Wood, 'you are a very peculiar people in Portobello!'. Since things had reached an impasse, the Town Council agreed to withdrawal of the clause so objectionable to Lord Redesdale, and entered into a binding agreement with Bouch that there should be no activities on Sundays. Sabbatarians in Scotland were a force to be reckoned with, as the early railway companies had discovered.

The pier was completed in 1871, although by that time the cost had risen to £10,000, the extra being found by Bouch and his backers. The formal opening took place on 23 May 1871, and appears to have been favoured with fair weather. There was a procession of all the local dignitaries from the Town Hall to the Pier, where they were welcomed by Provost Wood, who declared the pier open in an appropriate speech. Lord Provost Law of Edinburgh, Provost Watt of Leith and Provost Sanderson of Musselburgh, accompanied by their Magistrates, together with many lesser burghers, embarked on a steamer at the pierhead for a cruise on the Forth. Returning to the Pier Saloon, where a generous lunch awaited them, a good time was had by all and the champagne flowed freely. Strangely, or perhaps typically, nowhere in the reports is there any mention of the presence of Bouch himself. On such occasions he was liable to find urgent business elsewhere.

The pier was of quite light construction, of cast and wrought iron with timber decks, and carried on screw piles driven deep into the sand of the foreshore. This system had been used successfully by Bouch for other works on soft ground where conventional piling had failed. The beach at Portobello slopes gradually, and to obtain sufficient depth of water for steamers the pier had to be taken out 1,250ft from the shore. At deck level it was originally 22ft wide, except for 170ft at the pierhead where it broadened out to accommodate the large Pier Saloon, where refreshments were served and entertainments held, weather of course permitting.

For nearly twenty years the pier was a modest financial success, the Company paying regular dividends. Recurring storm damage made it expensive to maintain, and after the death of Bouch in 1880, Lady Bouch sold it off to a Mr M.P. Galloway, the proprietor of a fleet of pleasure steamers, for the sum of £1,500. Finally in 1892 Galloway sold out to the North British Railway who maintained the pier until 1915 when an unusually severe storm caused serious damage. Under wartime conditions repair was not contemplated, and in 1916 it was demolished with the scrap going to feed the war effort. In 1939 there were grandiose plans for building a new pier with a thousand-seat concert hall and restaurant, finished by a clock tower above, visible from all parts of the promenade. These proposals died a natural death with the advent of war and were never revived.

5

MINOR LINES NORTH
OF THE FORTH

A full list of all railways in which Thomas Bouch played some part will be found in Appendix I. While a few of the more important lines will be dealt with at greater length, the minor lines will be grouped geographically, since any attempt to describe them chronologically would become very complicated. This chapter will describe those lines north of the Tay Estuary.

The Crieff Lines

In the early 1850s Crieff was a small and somewhat sleepy country town, with a population of around 4,500, being at that period the second largest town in Perthshire and a popular resort for tourists. The Scottish Central had reached Perth by 23 May 1848 but had bypassed Crieff by 12 miles. Various proposals were put forward to place Crieff on the railway map, but none had come to anything. Realising that they would need to take the matter into their own hands, the Town Council commissioned a survey by Thomas Bouch of the best route to join the Scottish Central Railway, and a Bill was submitted to Parliament in 1852, with the Royal Assent being given on 15 August 1853. Thomas Bouch was appointed engineer, and the chosen route was to run to Crieff Junction (now better known as Gleneagles).

By the summer of 1854 there was little sign of any work being done, and Bouch complained that pressure of business prevented his attendance at meetings. When he did at last attend in March 1855, he was almost frogmarched by two directors to examine faults on the line. At a meeting in July, Bouch once more failed to attend, and it was disclosed that the SCR had not received the plans for the new junction, and the contractor was pressing for payment of nearly £5,000 because Bouch had failed to produce the warrant for payment. It was reported that Bouch had taken the warrant to the March meeting, and then had gone home with it in his pocket. So the sorry tale went on, but pressure on Bouch at last resulted in a firm undertaking to have the railway open by September 1855. The recruitment of staff was optimistically started. There was more trouble to come, and in consequence no work for the newly recruited staff, many of whom looked elsewhere for work and had to be replaced.

In January 1856 Bouch declared the line ready for its Board of Trade inspection. Still some work remained to be completed, and Gowans, the contractor, refused to attend to it until he was paid, while Bouch refused to pay, as he was entitled to do, until the work was finished. However, they settled their differences, and by 13 March the Board of Trade was satisfied, though not the SCR who demanded improvements to be made to the pointwork at Crieff Junction, which Gowans undertook to do.

Unfortunately the Company had given great offence to Lady Willoughby d'Eresby, the leading landowner around Crieff, because they had refused to build her a private station, and it was found out too late that she controlled all the possible sources of water needed for the locomotives. Her ladyship would not give way for it seems that her pride rather than her pocket was involved, even though, under duress, the railway would have paid well. Eventually, faced with no other option, the Company was driven to digging a deep well within the station precincts, and only then could the public service commence.

The railway soon led to more tourists and, to accommodate these, two hydropathic establishments were constructed where visitors could apply the local mineral waters both internally and externally. Similar establishments were springing up at other 'spa' towns, such as Moffat and Peebles, attempting to emulate their far more numerous and famous opposite numbers on the Continent. It was generally considered that the more foul smelling and tasting the waters were, the more beneficial were their properties.

The Perth, Almond Valley & Methven Railway

This short branch, 6½ miles in length, was built from the Scottish Midland Junction Railway just north of Perth, and received its Act in 1856, opening two and a half years later. In the summer a coach provided an onward service to Crieff, but there was agitation in the town for a railway to link Crieff with Methven and thus obtain a direct line to Perth. Although there is no record of Bouch having played any part in the original Almond Valley branch, the report by Captain Tyler RE was highly critical and it was the end of December 1858 before the line was allowed to open.

With the new line from Crieff proposed, Bouch came into the picture once again, but on this occasion there are no reports of serious problems. Like many, but not all, of these small railways, they lived hand to mouth and were absorbed into the ever expanding empire of the Caledonian Railway within a few years. The Crieff & Methven was the last to lose its independence in 1869.

The Blairgowrie and Kirriemuir Branches

These two small branches were built by the Scottish Midland Junction Railway after completion of its main line along Strathmore from Perth to Forfar, and were intended to act as feeders to the main line. At this time Bouch was a freelance consulting engineer and not yet consulting engineer to the North British (it is uncertain if he was ever formally appointed by the NBR) and in consequence happy to take on any commissions that came his way.

The Scottish Midland Junction Railway ran on an almost level alignment up the Vale of Strathmore, and reached Forfar, a busy town with a population of about 11,000, on 20 August 1848, passing through Coupar Angus on the way. The original Act had included the branches to Blairgowrie and Kirriemuir, but after five years when no start had been made a new Act was needed. Probably it was at this juncture that Bouch was called in to make a survey, prepare a Bill, and nurse it through Parliament.

A Mr Mitchell, probably appointed and paid by Bouch, was recorded as being the resident engineer. It was just west of Coupar Angus that the branch to Blairgowrie left the main line, crossed the river Isla on a twelve-span timber viaduct, and turned northwards towards its terminus some 5 miles distant. There was one intermediate station at Rosemount, and, small though it was, it boasted its own stationmaster.

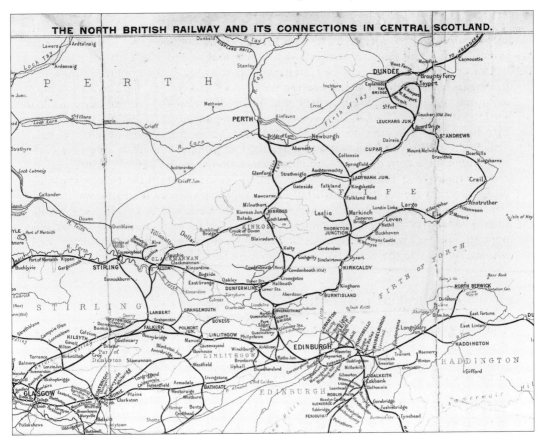

Official map of the North British Railway in Central Scotland.

Blairgowrie was a small town, with some industry powered from the waters of the Ericht, but its principal importance was derived from its position at the centre of a fertile agricultural area, renowned for its soft fruit, particularly raspberries. There were schemes to extend the line northwards but they came to nothing since the Highland Railway had built its main line through Blair Atholl, and the lie of the land north of Blairgowrie through Glen Ericht would have made construction expensive and with very limited local traffic to be had. In the early years there was no turntable at Blairgowre and only tank engines were authorised to work the branch. Both engine crews and BOT Inspectors disliked running tender first for good reason.

Apart from the viaduct across the Isla there were no engineering works of any consequence. When Locke and Errington had driven the line from Perth to Aberdeen, there were no iron bridges the whole way and masonry bridges were the norm wherever possible. This arose from Locke's strong prejudice against cast iron for bridgeworks, and even wrought iron was viewed only as a last resort. This resulted in a number of timber bridges which the Caledonian was later obliged to replace at considerable cost, the last meeting its end in 1888. Since Bouch had worked for four years with Locke as his mentor and timber bridges were initially much cheaper to construct – a factor which always weighed heavily with Bouch – he naturally chose timber for the Isla viaduct, untreated, as was his custom, which with hindsight seems a false economy. On more than one occasion Bouch was guilty of spending a shilling to save sixpence, even on the Tay Bridge.

Above: The harbour at Leven with private owner wagons of the Fife Coal Co. waiting to be discharged into coastal colliers. The limited size of the harbour led to much congestion as the coal trade rapidly increased, and an extensive new harbour was built.

Left: Captain Sir Henry Whatley Tyler KCB. Appointed a Railway Inspector in 1853, he was sent to inspect Bouch's Leven Railway. He was Chief Inspector from 1871–77 when he resigned and became Chairman of the Westinghouse Brake Co. (UK).

The small goods yard at Leslie. The main source of traffic was coal and raw materials to the paper mills, and export of the finished products. All traffic, amounting to many thousands of tons annually, now has to go by road.

The twelve spans were each about 30ft in the clear, and there is a strong probability that they consisted of laminated timber arches, which Locke had used extensively on the main line. This was a very economical but strong form of construction when new, but tended to have a short life because sooner or later water penetrated between the laminations leading to timber rot. When examined in 1865 it was given a clean bill of health. However the viaduct was beginning to feel its age sixteen years later when in February 1881 there was a particularly hard frost covering the river in thick ice. As the ice melted it threatened to destroy the viaduct, and all night Caledonian workers were engaged in breaking up the ice. Came the dawn and the viaduct still stood but more shaky than ever. The Caledonian ordered its immediate replacement by an iron lattice girder bridge.

The Blairgowrie branch, at the beginning, had a feature not enjoyed by other lines, and that was a signalling system which was the brainchild of Bouch himself. He had wanted to install it on the Leven Railway, but had been rebuffed. Signalling on all lines was still primitive where it existed at all, and the view of management was that signals made enginemen inattentive to their duties. It was customary to use colour to indicate the position of the signal arm, coupled with coloured lights at night. Colour blindness in drivers posed a problem when it was recognised, and a positive danger in milder cases where it might pass unnoticed. Colour blindness exercised the minds of Victorian savants, from the lowly Robert H. Bow up to the great James Clerk-Maxwell. Bouch's system avoided the use of colour. It gave three indications by day, repeated in the dark by white lights and the relative positions of the arms indicated the state of the line ahead. It does not appear to have been copied elsewhere, but a fuller description is listed in the bibliography.

The handsome viaduct over the Leven Valley on the approach to Leslie Station. It now provides a well-used public footpath.

John Haigs' distillery at Cameron Bridge on the Leven Railway which can be seen passing on the left. This is from an invoice heading and is dated 1879. Haig was a major supporter of the construction of the line and provided much traffic.

The Kirriemuir branch was only 3 miles in length, and left the main Strathmore line at Kirriemuir Junction, between Glamis and Forfar, and beyond the point where the main line had crossed the river Isla thus avoiding a bridge. Kirriemuir was a small town with a population of about 7,500 at the time the line opened on 20 November 1854; its main industry was jute weaving and there were also a couple of meal mills. It was the centre of a rich agricultural area, and specialised in the export of seed potatoes. It is perhaps most widely known as the birthplace of the playwright Sir James Barrie, which in the course of time led to increased tourist traffic, though in the 1890 *Baedeker's Guide* it had not developed sufficiently to be mentioned. The line did not present any engineering problems.

The Arbroath & Montrose Railway

This forms part of the East Coast line from Kings Cross to Aberdeen and deserves a chapter of its own, particularly with the sad saga of the first South Esk Viaduct at Montrose. Bouch had died before its completion.

Lines in the Kingdom of Fife: The Leven Railway and the East of Fife Railway
The St Andrews Railway, which launched the career of Thomas Bouch as a consulting civil engineer, is dealt with separately. Descriptions will in general be restricted to those of greatest interest. Nonetheless, large and small, all contributed to the growth and success of the Scottish rural economy for a century until overtaken by inevitable change.

While the St Andrews Railway was under construction it aroused the interest of persons at the small port of Leven on the Fife coast, where there was some industry, and the hinterland was a prosperous farming area. A single line of economical construction was proposed from Thornton on the EP&D to the small harbour at Leven, a distance of 6 miles. Landowners along the route proved from the start to be almost as grasping and intransigent as their opposite numbers south of the Border, and were the source of many disputes which delayed the construction. The only intermediate station was at Cameron Bridge where there was a large distillery owned by John Haig, who became Chairman of the Company. Fortunately, the line was able to follow two river valleys and the earthworks were light. Who better than Bouch to be the engineer? Rumours of problems on the St Andrews Railway had apparently not yet reached the Leven area. The rhetorical answer might be 'almost anybody', for when the line was opened the new locomotive, ordered by Bouch from Hawthorns of Leith, was delivered late and full of faults. Similarly, the thirty wagons ordered from a Birmingham firm also proved defective.

This was only the tip of the iceberg. When the Leven contractor moved to install the new connection to the EP&D he was sent packing as Bouch had failed to provide the necessary plans. Bouch did not attend a Board meeting when summoned by the Secretary. On 24 May 1853 Bouch was ordered by the Board to complete negotiations with the EP&D. Eight months later nothing had happened, and the Board expressed their frustration in the Minutes and sent a copy to Bouch.

When the line was inspected by Captain Tyler RE on 2 August 1854, the Inspector reported, with reference to the Parliamentary survey, that the curves were too sharp and the gradients too steep, while the ballasting was inadequate and entirely missing in places. Despite this, approval was given for the railway to open on 7 August. Tyler had only been appointed the year before at the age of twenty-six and John Haig probably assured him that the necessary work would be put in hand forthwith. The saga of the new locomotive is too long to repeat here, but it nearly brought the Company to its knees. Finally, in desperation the Directors wrote Bouch yet another letter, the last paragraph of which read:

The substantial station at Crieff built to serve the heavy tourist traffic and the two hydropathic establishments. The first connection was to what is now Gleneagles and a link to Perth via Methven opened ten years later.

The station at Kinross Junction, where the Fife & Kinross, the Devon Valley, and the Kinross-shire Railways met. In later years this offered an alternative route from West Fife to Perth. Queen Victoria passed through here after crossing the Tay Bridge in 1879.

The Directors, I can assure you, have taken up this matter with great pain and reluctance, but as has been seen, while implicitly trusting you, they have been grievously disappointed in the deficiencies accidentally discovered in the works of the railway and they feel that they have the very strongest claims on you for relief from the consequences.

Perhaps they were paying the price for their reluctance to attend Board meetings and leaving everything to Wilkie.

Within a few years the Leven Railway proved to be highly profitable, paying as much as 8% in dividends. The Directors sensed that an extension along the east coast could also prove equally profitable; they were mostly local landowners with a greater interest in future dividends than in the grind of supervising the building of a railway. As a result Bouch was left very much to his own devices, with the Company Secretary, Wilkie, a local lawyer, dealing with administration but possessing no engineering knowledge. Thus it would seem that problems never came to the ears of the Directors during the earlier stages of the line, and they retained a misplaced trust in their engineer.

While work on the Leven Railway was underway, the East of Fife Railway was proposed, to extend from Leven along the Fife coast, initially to Kilconquhar, a distance of 12½ miles, but there was talk of eventually reaching St Andrews from the south. Bouch was commissioned to survey the first stage as far as Kilconquhar, and had completed this and produced an estimate, when rumours of problems with the Leven survey became known after Captain Tyler's inspection. The East of Fife Directors immediately ordered a fresh survey to be made by another engineer, which disclosed many errors in Bouch's survey. He was immediately dismissed, and a young engineer of the name of Martin, who had been working for Bouch on one of his lines in Perthshire, was appointed in his place.

This was the third survey found to be at fault including the St Andrews and Leven previously. It appears amazing that Bouch could get away with it for so long without prejudicing his reputation. Since he had been well trained by George Larmer on the Lancaster & Carlisle it seems due more to bad business organisation rather than plain incompetence – a failure to pay strict attention to business as Wilkie had found out on the Leven. That unfortunate man had struggled to get his Directors and Bouch in the same place at the same time. Instead of relying on competent, paid assistants, Bouch preferred to delegate responsibilities to unpaid pupils, whose parents parted with substantial premiums to have their sons trained. When it came to surveying they were sent out on their own to gain practical experience without supervision. No other explanation seems to fit the bill but it remains conjecture.

The Leslie Railway

An Act was passed on 7 July 1857 for the construction of a railway from Markinch Junction, on the EP&D main line, to the small manufacturing town of Leslie, now absorbed into Glenrothes New Town. In 1846 the E&N, as it then was, had proposed such a line, but received strong opposition from Lord Rothes over the next ten years, with various alternative routes proposed and discarded. His lordship finally gave in and agreed not to oppose a Bill which was placed before Parliament. The unfortunate effect was that not only did a roundabout route result, but two expensive stone viaducts over the river Leven could not be avoided. The engineering works were heavy for a line of only 6¼ miles in all.

On leaving Markinch Junction, the first siding was to John Haig's whisky bottling plant. Beyond was Auchmuty Junction, where the Auchmuty minerals only branch descended into the Leven Valley to serve the paper mills of Grossett & Dixon and Tullis Russell. The

Leslie line started climbing to pass over the Balbirnie Viaduct of ten round-headed arches. Shortly before reaching Leslie Station the line passed over the elegant Leslie Viaduct of fourteen semi-elliptical spans, an arch form uncommon in Scotland, and the only one credited to Bouch. Both viaducts still stand, the Leslie is one now used as a footpath. From Leslie goods yard a short branch served the Fettykil Paper Mills of Smith, Anderson & Co. Although still producing 50,000 tons of paper annually, all traffic to and from the mill now has to go by road. At Leslie also were the Strathendry Paper Mills of J.A. Weir Ltd, and adjacent to the Station there was a textile works. The line opened for passenger traffic on 1 February 1861, when the population of Leslie stood at about 4,300, and the line was eventually acquired by the NBR on 1 August 1872.

The Lines to Kinross

By the time Bouch arrived in Edinburgh, the Edinburgh & Northern Railway had employed Grainger & Miller to build the main lines across Fife from Burntisland on the north bank of the Forth to Ladybank. From there it branched eastwards to Ferryport-on-Craig (later Tayport) from where there was a ferry service to Broughty Ferry, and thence to Dundee via the Dundee & Arbroath Railway. The westerly branch from Ladybank reached Perth by a junction with the Scottish Central Railway at Hilton Junction, the last mile being over SMR track where the EP&D intrusion was not always welcome.

To develop the rural areas of Fife, Bouch's philosophy of cheap or economical railways came into its own. Lightly built single lines involving the minimum of earthworks and bridges could be constructed for less than £6,000 a mile compared with six times as much for a conventional double-track main line. The town of Kinross had a population of about 2,500. The first line to reach the town was the Fife & Kinross Railway, which received its Act in July 1855, with Thomas Bouch as engineer. This was to run from Ladybank to Kinross, a distance of 14 miles, and provision was made for a possible extension down the Devon Valley to meet the SMR branch from Alloa to Tillicoultry. It would be some years before the Devon Valley extension was completed due to the expense and difficulty of traversing the Devon Gorge between Rumbling Bridge and Tillicoultry.

From the south the Kinross-shire Railway, which received its Act two years later in 1857, again with Thomas Bouch as engineer, was to run from Cowdenbeath and Kelty, through the Blairadam Forest and along the southern side of Loch Leven. The district attracted many summer visitors and the loch was renowned for its trout fishing and for winter skating and curling. Trains would stop specially to unload the heavy curling stones, but passengers had to walk from the nearest station. Apart from this the traffic on both lines was mainly local. The line from Kinross to Rumbling Bridge, a distance of 6 miles, followed the open valley of the Gelly Burn before descending into the valley of the Devon. Having been opened to Rumbling Bridge on 1 May 1863, there it stopped for eight years, for the last 4 miles to Tillicoultry passed through the Devon gorge involving heavy engineering works, and it was 1 May 1871 before this final link was completed. It was probably only the first 6 miles from Kinross that were the responsibility of Bouch, for his energies towards the end of the 1860s were mainly to be taken up with the Tay Bridge.

The Tay Bridge Approach and the Newport Railway

The southern approach to the Tay Bridge left the original main line to Tayport at Leuchars, and the last station before the bridge was at St Fort. Here it was customary to collect all tickets from passengers ending their journeys at Dundee. Those proceeding beyond Dundee on the Dundee & Arbroath Joint Line would retain their tickets, and as a result the attempt to arrive at a definite count of those lost when the bridge fell could at best be only an estimate pending the finding of bodies or reports of missing persons from anxious friends and relatives.

The village of Newport, on the south bank of the Tay facing Dundee, was chosen by a number of businessmen from the city to build their houses in the cleaner air of Fife. There were two problems which prevented a more rapid expansion. The most serious was the very limited supply of fresh water, but the state of the ferries was also a long-standing source of complaints which the owners, the Scottish Central Railway, chose to ignore. Of one ferry, the *Newport*, it was reported that 'in the fore and aft cabins the smell of bilge water is so obnoxious as to render them intolerable'. After the SCR had been absorbed into the Caledonian empire conditions started to improve. For nearly a year after the Tay Bridge had opened in 1878, Newport was still unable to enjoy a rail service to Dundee, but the provision of a 6in water main over the bridge was widely welcomed. Finally, on 12 May 1879 the first train ran through from Tayport to Dundee. Naturally William McGonagall celebrated the occasion:

> The thrifty housewives of Newport
> To Dundee will often resort
> Which will be to them profit and sport,
> By bringing cheap tea, bread and jam
> And also some of Lipton's ham.

With the opening of the bridge and the branch through Newport the number of passengers using the ferries dropped off sharply, but they continued to run to cater for those of a nervous disposition who feared to use the bridge, and there was quite a number who were deterred initially by the various doom-mongers who foretold its destruction. Within eight months the ferries were once again resurrected for full service after the bridge fell in a gale.

6

MINOR LINES TO THE SOUTH OF EDINBURGH

The Peebles Railway

The NBR Hawick Branch opened on 1 November 1849. The chosen route over Falahill and down the valley of the Gala Water to Galashiels was the shortest, though involving much hard going, and the alternative route to Peebles and down the Tweed Valley was considerably longer and offered few advantages. Peebles was a small town on the banks of the Tweed famous for its fishing which attracted many visitors, while the woollen industry offered year-round employment. From an industrial aspect it was off the beaten track, being over 20 miles south of Edinburgh, at a time when road improvements lay in the future. A railway connection would have reduced the cost of coal for the mills and the export of finished products, and easier access would have attracted more visitors and even commuters from Edinburgh. There was great disappointment in the town when it was bypassed by the railway to Hawick.

The businessmen of the town and its hoteliers and other interested parties set up a provisional committee to investigate providing a railway to Edinburgh, but an engineer was needed. The secretary, John Bathgate, reported favourably on one Thomas Bouch, stating that:

> The Committee, having ascertained that Mr Thomas Bouch CE had turned his attention to the construction of railways in an economical manner and had successfully completed a branch to St Andrews at a cheap rate, and having also otherwise reason to be satisfied with his zeal, integrity, and professional attainments, resolved to employ him.

This was to turn out an example of how satisfactorily Bouch's light railways could be built. The reason was not far to seek. The Directors were hard-headed men of business; they knew what they wanted and were determined to receive value for their money. By 8 July 1853 they had their Act.

The Peebles line left the NBR at Hardengreen Junction, near Eskbank, and was single, except for passing places, all the way to Peebles. So it remained until closure in February 1962, after more than a century of public service. In its earlier years it proved to be highly profitable too. Although the area was not thickly populated, there were seven stations in its 18¾ miles. One originally named Penicuik purported to serve the village of the name, but to reach the station by road involved a steep descent into the valley of the North Esk and an equally steep climb on the far side. Once the real Penicuik Railway had arrived the station was renamed Pomathorn.

When opened on 4 July 1855 the management of the line was delegated to a professional Manager, assisted by a locomotive superintendent, John Blackwood, enticed away from the Caledonian. There had been earlier discussions with the NBR but terms could not be agreed, and the use of a railway operating contractor who would supply everything from staff to tickets was seriously considered. This was quite a common practice on small railways, though not without problems on both sides. A firm was chosen, but when offered a contract replied that they were too busy. In the end it was back to direct labour at the recommendation of John Bathgate. Bouch had been sent out to report on the working of several small railways, and although he favoured the system of the Kendal & Windermere, worked by the LNWR, Bathgate opposed copying such a large organisation which had a different approach with a vast, centralised management. Inevitably, in 1861 the Directors bowed to the blandishments of Richard Hodgson of the NBR and his empire building, and the line was leased to the bigger company. In 1876 it was formally absorbed into the NBR.

There were no engineering works of any magnitude, but a rise of about 600ft between Hardengreen and the summit at Leadburn had to be overcome, and from there the line fell about 500ft to Peebles. This resulted in a ruling gradient of up to 1:53 or 1:60 which did not make for easy working, but was tolerable on an 'economical' line. Initially there was a modest station and goods yard at Peebles, but this was replaced by a handsome new station by 1866 with the opening of the extension to Innerleithen and Galashiels. Early in 1858, after dragging their heels for some months, Peebles and intermediate stations were linked to the NBR electric telegraph system at Hardengreen and thence to Edinburgh. Use of the system was made available to the public for sending messages, at a fee of course.

The contract for the building of the line was awarded to Bray & Dyson, but did not include the supply of rails, and Bouch considered their subsequent tender for rails too high. He negotiated with the NBR for the supply of 2,200 tons of used main line rails in 16ft lengths, delivered at Hardengreen for £7 7s a ton. This was £2 3s a ton less than Bray & Dyson had quoted for rails of similar weight but presumably new. Economy ruled, and in the longer term the NBR rails, which were life expired on the main line, had to be replaced at considerable expense after they took over. It is arguable that this policy was false economy, but it did allow rural lines to be built when capital was short and revenues would not service a large debt. It was applied by Brunel with his timber viaducts in Devon and Cornwall, and by Locke with timber bridges on the line to Aberdeen.

Branches off the Peebles Railway soon appeared. These were (a) the Esk Valley Railway, (b) the Penicuik Railway, (c) the Leadburn, Linton and Dolphinton Railway, while the Loanhead, Roslin and Glencorse was another Bouch line in close proximity.

The Esk Valley Railway

Perhaps more generally known as the Polton Branch, this was another small branch in the area south of Edinburgh which was primarily intended to serve local industry in the valley of the river North Esk, south of Lasswade. It possessed one feature, rare on a Bouch line, in having a tunnel 430 yards in length.

It was authorised as an independent company under the Esk Valley Railway Act of 21 July 1863. Construction started in September 1864 but it was not until 12 April 1867 that the line was ready for inspection by the Board of Trade. The formal opening for traffic took place three days later. It is unclear why it should have taken two and a half years to build such a short line, but possibly there were problems with the tunnel or even difficulties in raising the capital of £27,000.

The single line branched off from the Peebles Railway, still independent at that period, at Esk Valley Junction. The first station before the tunnel was Broomieknow, preceded by a short-lived siding to Polton Colliery. Descending on a gradient of 1:50 through the tunnel, the line emerged high up on the side of the Esk Valley at Lasswade Station. At Lasswade was situated the long-established St Leonard's Paper Mill and a gas works belonging to the Lasswade & Bonnyrigg Gas Light Co.

Beyond Lasswade Station the line descended at 1:50 into the bottom of the Esk Valley, and crossed the river on a six-arch stone viaduct. The first siding served Kevock Colliery, then came a siding to Kevock Paper Mill and the river was again crossed on a two-span cast-iron girder bridge. Then came two sidings to Polton Paper Mill, and another to the Springfield Paper Mill, and finally Polton Station was reached, at a distance of 2.63 miles from Esk Valley Junction.

From the start the line was worked by an agreement with the NBR and was legally absorbed by that company on 13 July 1871. The last goods train ran on 18 May 1964.

The Leadburn, Linton & Dolphinton Railway

This was a railway which in terms of potential traffic ran from nowhere to nowhere, and Bouch exercised the strictest economy ever. Its Act was passed on 3 June 1862 and it was 10 miles in length through an exclusively rural area. The opening took place on 4 July 1864 after an official inspection by Colonel Rich RE a fortnight previously. The inspection did not go entirely well. The Inspector was concerned at the lightness of the cast-iron chairs, and when several were weighed they turned the scales at an average of under 20lb each, compared with about 50lb for a standard chair. The lesson of St Andrews had been ignored, and any but the lightest of locomotives would lead to breakages, especially in cold weather. To crown the proceedings, the locomotive and test train, with Bouch and Colonel Rich on the footplate, broke through a cast-iron girder bridge. Bouch blamed this on a bad casting, which was probably true, for cast iron was an unreliable material at the best of times. But it was cheap!

The station at Linton was renamed Broomlee at the request of the NBR to avoid confusion with their East Linton station on the line to Berwick. Leadburn was the site of the most serious accident on the Peebles Railway. In October 1863, while the Dolphinton branch was under construction, a number of loaded wagons on the branch broke free, ran down a 1:67 gradient, and broke through the NBR stop block before running out on to the main line. An express from Edinburgh was due and met the runaway wagons head on. Despite great destruction, the only death was that of a small boy. Bouch's previous recommendation that proper catch points should be installed had been ignored by the NBR management.

The main source of traffic at Dolphinton was from seasonal sheep sales, and provision for passengers was only a wooden shed, primitive even by NBR standards. In 1862, when the Bill was before Parliament, there had been strenuous objections by the Caledonian, arguing that the line was intended to spearhead an intrusion by the NBR into their territory, but as they did not then have a line within 10 miles their objections were discounted and the Act was passed. In 1867 the Caledonian built a line from Carstairs to Dolphinton, which made an end-on connection with the NBR and blocked any expansion westwards by the latter. Since the two companies could not agree on a joint station each provided their own, but 500 yards apart. The NBR station closed on 1 April 1933.

Peebles NB Station was originally a modest affair which later became a goods shed. With the opening of the line to Galashiels and rapid development of the tourist and commuter traffic, as well as the opening of the Peebles Hydro, this commodious station was erected, albeit with only one platform.

The Firth Viaduct on the Penicuik branch where the line descends into the valley of the North Esk and crosses from east to west and, shortly after passing through a tunnel, crosses the Glencorse Burn on a bowstring girder bridge at Auchendinny.

The station and trussed bowstring girder bridge at Auchendinny, seen from the tunnel mouth. Bouch used this pattern of bridge extensively on the Cockermouth, Keswick & Penrith Railway but nowhere else in Scotland. The Tay Bridge bowstrings were different.

Penicuik Station looking south towards the Valleyfield Paper Mills beyond the road bridge. This was the NBR boundary and their locomotives were not allowed on to the private sidings beyond. Traffic in the mills had to be handled by horse power.

The station building at Penicuik appears to have been generously staffed. The small goods shed is to the right, and the tall chimney of Cowan's Paper Mill is visible in the background.

Penicuik Station looking towards Edinburgh. The Valleyfield Paper Mill and the water lade originally supplying their power can be seen on the left, and the chimney of the boiler house on the right among the trees.

Bonnyrigg Station, the first stop on the Peebles line after leaving the main Waverley route.

A fairly modern view of Gilmerton Colliery, though disused for many years. When passenger services ran to Roslin and Glencorse, Gilmerton was the first station after Millerhill and a short distance from the village.

The Victoria Viaduct, east of Dalkeith. This is included because no photograph of Bouch's viaduct at Bilston Glen can be found, but the construction is similar to an old NBR drawing of the first Bilston viaduct except the Bilston spans were shorter.

Leadburn Station on the Peebles line in 1962, looking south towards Peebles. The branch to Dolphinton left the main line about half a mile beyond the station

Polton Station and goods yard, terminus of the short Esk Valley Railway which branched off the Peebles railway at Hawthornden. The chimney of one of the paper mills served can be seen behind the row of cottages on the right.

When the Esk Valley Railway descended into the valley of the North Esk through a tunnel, immediately on leaving the tunnel was Lasswade Station and some distance from the village of that name, though it served some local industry and a gas works.

The NBR terminus and engine shed at Dolphinton. The connecting spur to the Caledonian Station ran behind the engine shed, but there was little through goods traffic with much of it going by way of Peebles.

Broomlee Station, roughly halfway between Leadburn and Dolphinton, served the village of West Linton. This was renamed from plain Linton because the NBR station at East Linton on the Berwick main line caused confusion.

The west end of Waverley Station after its reconstruction in the early 1870s. The new roof and the new Waverley Bridge in the foreground were the work of Thomas Bouch. The long-standing congestion on the western approach lines continues.

The Penicuik Railway

The primary purpose of this branch was to serve the population of Penicuik and its papermaking industry in the valley of the North Esk. The Penicuik Railway was 4½ miles in length, and received its Act on 20 June 1870 and opened on 9 May 1872. The intermediate stations were at Rosslyn (renamed Rosslyn Castle to distinguish it from Roslin on the Glencorse branch) and Auchendinny. The only other industry of note was a gunpowder works powered by the spark-free source of the river.

Arrival of the railway with its fire-breathing steam engines was a matter of some concern to the gunpowder makers at Rosslyn Castle, who insisted that the railway company should erect a corrugated iron shed, like a snowshed, to trap any sparks. The works survived until after the Second World War, apparently without a serious accident. By that time it had turned to producing high explosives and was part of the ICI organisation. Much of its output went away by road as there was a steep climb to the railway, but the NBR did supply special gunpowder vans when required.

Beyond Rosslyn Castle the railway descended the steep eastern side of the valley, which it crossed by a ten-arch stone viaduct and a cast-iron girder bridge over a farm road. Here the river entered a narrow gorge, with almost vertical rock face, through which the railway tunnelled, emerging directly on to a bowstring girder bridge over the river at Auchendinny, a small village with its own paper mill. Though smaller, this bridge closely resembles those used by Bouch on the Cockermouth, Keswick and Penrith line through the gorge of the Greta several years before, and may have come from the same Gilkes Wilson works at Middlesbrough. Beyond this the line again crossed the river twice on cast-iron girder bridges and entered Penicuik, where it served several paper mills. Being close to the village the station was more conveniently situated than the station on the Peebles line which was reluctantly renamed Pomathorn to avoid confusion. Passenger trains ceased to Polton and Penicuik in September 1951.

The Edinburgh, Loanhead & Roslin Railway

This line was built to serve the extensive mineral area lying to the south of Edinburgh, as well as the villages of Loanhead and Roslin. It received its Act on the same day as the Penicuik Railway, 20 June 1870, but this is the only connection since the ELRR left the NBR Hawick branch at Millerhill, rather nearer to Edinburgh than Eskbank and Hardengreen Junction for the Peebles Railway. The original proposal to extend the line to Penicuik was withdrawn to avoid a Parliamentary battle, and as a result the Penicuik Railway offered no opposition.

The principal beneficiaries of the new line would be the Shotts Iron Co. of Morningside in Lanarkshire, who mined extensively for coal and ironstone near the proposed line, but other industrial enterprises for the production of limestone and shale oil would also benefit. The Shotts Iron Co. had worked out the coal and ironstone near their works, and were forced to go further afield to obtain their supplies from the relatively undeveloped sources in Midlothian.

The supervision of the survey and construction was entrusted to Thomas Bouch, but pressure of work on the Tay Bridge obliged him to delegate the duty to his senior assistant, George Trimble. John Waddell of Bathgate, a contractor of good standing and trusted by Bouch, was the successful tenderer. As on the Peebles line trackwork was obtained second-hand from the NBR at a worthwhile saving.

After leaving Millerhill the line served Gilmerton Colliery and proceeded towards Loanhead. Before reaching Loanhead Station the Straiton Sidings, a purely mineral branch, led off to the west. These served the limeworks and the extensive oil shale workings and refinery. The Ramsey Pit adjoined the station, at Loanhead, then the line burrowed under the town centre and a branch to the former Boroughlee Colliery swung off to the right, while the main line to Roslin crossed the deep valley of the Bilston Burn on a six-span girder viaduct with 60ft lattice girders on masonry piers, the highest of which was 150ft. Reaching Roslin Station, a siding to Roslin Colliery, worked by the Glasgow Iron Co., continued for a short distance.

The Bilston Viaduct had a short but interesting history. If a later NBR drawing showing its proposed replacement is correct, the girders were not of R.H. Bow design with X bracing, always adopted by Bouch, but closely resemble the Victoria Viaduct at Dalkeith designed by Charles Jopp of the NBR. It may be that again pressure of work forced delegation of the design. By 1890 the Bilston Viaduct was threatened by mine workings, and a scheme by the NBR to replace it with a vast embankment was refused on amenity grounds. A pillar of coal costing £25,000 was paid for by the NBR, but fears as to the stability of the piers caused them to replace it shortly afterwards with the present fine structure, Listed Category A.

On 5 August 1872 the Act was received for the Glencorse extension. Continuing from Roslin, the line ran under the Auchendinny road before reaching the valley of the Glencorse Burn which was crossed by a brick viaduct of fifteen arches over the golf course. Recently, when loose bricks started falling on to the course, demolition had been deemed necessary. Glencorse Station stood facing the large Glencorse Barracks, and here passenger services terminated. Coal was loaded here for some years from the Greenlaw Colliery. A mineral branch extended towards Penicuik, with sidings to the Mauricewood Colliery, and passed under the main road to the Penicuik gas works. Further on at Eastfield attempts to sink a shaft failed due to excessive water, and a coal depot was established.

After a final BOT inspection by Major Hutchinson RE (who later as Major–General inspected the Tay Bridge), the line opened through to Glencorse on 2 July 1877. The distance from Millerhill to Eastfield was about 9 miles.

7

WORKS CARRIED OUT BY THOMAS BOUCH
IN THE NORTH OF ENGLAND

Successful completion of the Wear Valley Railway did not pass unnoticed by John Dixon, Chief Engineer of the S&D, who had a suitable job in mind for Bouch once the ill effects of the Railway Mania had worn off.

The Newcastle & Carlisle Railway had been the first line to cross the northern Pennines, and it profited accordingly while its monopoly lasted. Many schemes were put forward for Pennine crossings further south, mostly ill-conceived for they ran through miles of difficult country, with little prospect of remunerative traffic. Of the six major schemes proposed during the Railway Mania of 1845/6, only one was authorised by Parliament, the Liverpool, Manchester & Newcastle Junction Railway, and that was as far as it ever went with not a yard of track being laid. Between South Durham and West Cumberland there was prospective traffic, and the S&D was ideally situated to exploit it.

The iron trade developed where iron ore and timber (for charcoal) were to be found, and as the forests were laid waste and ore supplies were worked out, the discovery that coke could replace charcoal and the existence of ironstone in the Coal Measures caused the industry to move. Among the areas to develop were Furness and West Cumberland, and South Durham and Cleveland. Cumberland had large deposits of high-grade haematite iron order, but the coal was not of good coking quality. Conversely Durham had the finest of coking coals, but was forced to rely on the low-grade ironstone of the Cleveland hills which, being soft in nature, clogged the blast furnaces and, with a much lower proportion of iron, was more expensive to smelt. A railway running directly between the east and west coasts was needed, to send coking coal to Cumberland and haematite ore to Durham.

John Dixon could see that the most direct route would be from Darlington, through Barnard Castle and over the Stainmore Forest to join the LNWR at Tebay, although the route from there to Furness would still be roundabout. Who better to send out to do a visual survey that young Bouch? So it came about that Bouch was provided with a horse and sent to tackle the wilderness. Bouch could not be described as inexperienced, but he clearly lacked Joseph Locke's expert eye, and the report that he submitted was highly optimistic as future experience would prove. Why he was sent over Stainmore in the middle of the winter is difficult to fathom, but in due course he reported to John Dixon:

Appleby. 27/1/1848. To John Dixon Esq. Dear Sir,
I intended writing to you earlier but only now have arrived at an opinion of the probable
character of the line you may expect through this part of the country. From Darlington
to the summit at Stainmore I expect our section will show a beautiful line. On this side
of Stainmore the ground is not so favourable. I have been rather unfortunate since I left
Darlington. I have lamed my left foot, and persevering with my work it got so much swollen
and inflamed that I was obliged to consult the doctor who leeched my left foot and gave me
a good deal of medicine, and ordered me to lay it up for a few days.

It is believed that Bouch had fallen off his horse, hardly surprising on such rough going,
but embarrassing to admit. There followed a further communication:

Darlington. 8/2/48. To John Dixon Esq. Dear Sir,
I have much pleasure in informing you that I have today discovered a new and much superior
route for the Lancashire branch … From the appearance of water in the becks the gradients
will be good. There will be no viaducts or tunnels, and the earthworks will be so light that I
have reason for thinking that the line will cost less per mile than the Weardale.

There is little doubt that to the end of his working life Bouch was an incurable optimist,
making light of problems which would daunt many other men. Even the Tay Bridge was
described as a 'very ordinary undertaking'. When he actually came to build the Stainmore
line several years later it was to prove no ordinary undertaking.

Although the S&D had weathered the Railway Mania years in much better shape than
many, the vast expenditure of capital, much of it of no useful purpose other than to line
the pockets of company promoters, crooked lawyers and shysters of every hue, meant that
it would be after 1850 before money became available for major new projects. Bouch's
report was shelved, but he had encountered no insuperable obstacles to constructing the
line. The Pennine weather was another matter when it came to operating it.

The years were passing, and Bouch did not lack ambition, so when towards the end
of 1848 the post of Manager of the Edinburgh & Northern Railway (since the middle
of 1847 it had become the Edinburgh, Perth & Dundee but the old name clung on) was
advertised, Bouch hastened to apply with the blessing of his employers. Despite intense
competition he was successful, and wrote to Edward Pease:

I have great pleasure in informing you that my application for the Managership of the
Edinburgh & Northern Railway [sic] has been successful notwithstanding that there were a
hundred applicants. I feel very much obliged to you and my other friends who favoured me
with the testimonials to whom I am entirely indebted for the appointment.

This did not mark an end to his association with the Stockton & Darlington, for in the
years to come he would not only undertake perhaps his greatest work, the Stainmore
line, but its continuation from Barnard Castle to Darlington (actually built first), and
the remarkably slim and handsome viaduct at Hownes Gill on the line to Consett – all
tributes to his skill. Now, after a few days break at Thursby, his great adventure was to start
at the behest of the Stockton & Darlington.

This trans-Pennine line was built in four main sections. The first ran from Darlington
to Barnard Castle, the second over the top to Tebay, a third from a junction at Kirkby
Stephen to Penrith, and a fourth to Cockermouth where it made an end-on junction
with the existing line to Workington and the West Cumberland industrial area. Because
the route from North Durham via Darlington was circuitous, a later connection was made
from Bishop Auckland to Barnard Castle, and near Penrith an avoiding curve was added
to save reversing at Penrith.

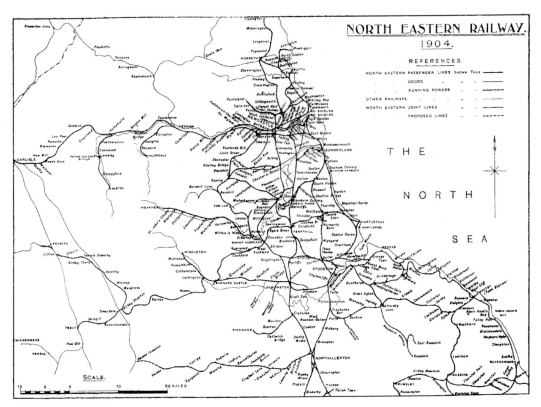

Official map of the North Eastern Railway, 1904.

The four main sections were built as follows:

Darlington to Barnard Castle	Act 3/7/1854	Opened 8/7/1856
South Durham & Lancashire Union (Barnard Castle to Tebay)	Act 13/7/1857	Opened 8/8/1861
Eden Valley, Kirkby Stephen to Clifton Junction LNWR	Act 21/5/1858	Opened 8/4/1862
Penrith to Cockermouth	Act 1/8/1861	Opened 2/1/1865

All the above lines were engineered by Thomas Bouch, and showed what he could achieve when free from the financial straightjacket imposed by the cheap railway policy. While he could never be accused of extravagance, his major works were dominated by a policy of value for money.

Above: The Deepdale Viaduct under construction. All parts were standardised for this and the Belah Viaduct, and prefabricated in Middlesbrough. Gilkes Wilson's erection team of eighty men was able to complete Deepdale in forty-seven days, with only the simple erecting gear shown.

Opposite: The curving trestle bridge at Deepdale on the Stainmore line. It appears that repainting is almost completed, although it was demolished within a few years. The painters have assured themselves of a place in posterity.

The Darlington & Barnard Castle Railway

The town of Barnard Castle was somewhat isolated, and by 1832 there was agitation for a railway. For the next twenty years schemes came and went without any progress on the ground. In 1853 a Bill before Parliament failed, but a second attempt the following year was successful. However, there was still opposition from the Duke of Cleveland, whose Raby Castle estate included much of the land east of Barnard Castle through which the railway would need to pass. Other landowners along the line of the proposed railway were reluctant to show any support until they could see which way His Grace intended to jump.

The first Duke of Cleveland had been an implacable opponent of railways in the north of Durham where he had his principal residence at Lambton Castle. The rapid expansion of railways and tramroads and the industrialisation of the countryside around Lambton drove him to move to his other estate at Raby Castle which had been left untouched by development. When he died in 1840 it was expected that his son, the second duke, would take a similar attitude. It is said that, to avoid any confrontation when on the Duke's land, Bouch dressed his surveyors as miners. Such subterfuges were not unknown in the early days of railways, but Bouch's men were caught red-handed, and Bouch was ordered to attend at Raby Castle in person to apologise to the Duke for this unauthorised incursion.

Bouch duly turned up at the castle, dressed in his best. To his relief he received a friendly welcome from the Duke who, for his part, was surprised at this smart, well-mannered and well-spoken young gentleman instead of the rough and ready working engineer he had expected. An amicable discussion followed, and unexpectedly the Duke promised to withdraw his opposition. Afterwards the smaller landowners followed suit. From an engineering point of view the work was straightforward with no large structures, and the line was completed in two years from the passing of the Act. A simple but handsome station was provided, but it was badly sited, and a new station had to be built when the Tebay line was constructed. The first station became a goods shed, and in 1862 was divided to form two houses.

Above: Deepdale Viaduct.

Left: William Randolph Innes Hopkins founded the Teeside Iron Works which merged with the Tees Engine Works in 1865. The firm then became Hopkins, Gilkes & Co. They tendered for the Tay Bridge and were awarded the contract after two other firms had failed.

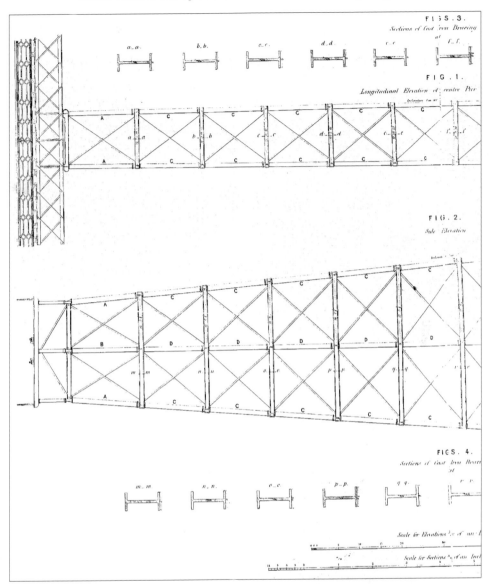

A contemporary drawing showing the girders and towers of the Deepdale and Belah viaducts built by Gilkes, Wilson & Co. of Middlesbrough. The designers were Thomas Bouch and Robert H. Bow. The latter became an authority on braced structures and graphical statics.

Beelah   Viaduct

On Stainmore, Westmoreland, the "Wonder of the Age!"

Dedicated to Thomas Bouch, Esq. C. E , by J. Close, Author of the "Book of the Chronicles," a "Month in London," "Adventures of an Author," "Wise Men of Gotham," (a Comic Drama in 3 Acts), the "Kirkby-Stephen Cricket Papers," "Bring Flowers," Wondrous Story of a Poet's Life, Priestcraft & Purgatory, Confessions of Simon Daisy, &c

Poet Close reading his Poem to Mr Bouch

O Wondrous Age ! a wondrous age we live in,
  When Stainmore echoes with an awful din:
What novel sounds the 80 men are giving,
  While fixing firm the Iron Pillars in.

Well may they come in crowds from ev'ry part
  The London Cockney and the Country Squire ;
Each rub their eyes—each throbbing swelling heart
  Expands, while lost in wonder all admire.

Well may they come, on foot on horseback riding
  In Carriages close pack'd here all the Quality ;
What shouts and noisy echoes rend the sky
  What slips and falls, what merry sociality !

Oh BOUCH ! what a prolific Brain is thine,
  To scheme at first this strange gigantic plan ;
Thine Eye could scan our rugged Hills and Vales
  Such Genius proves thee a superior man.

He said " It can, it must be done !" and lo !
  From Middlesbro' came forth the clever men
Who catch'd a spark of Bouch's electric fire
  And flashing Thought began its work again.

And shall Squire Wakefield's Name here be forgot ?
  To whom Westmeria owes much in praise ;
And our Squire Thompson also credit due
  His Thousands help'd this Viaduct to raise.

And gentle-hearted PEASE who went to soothe
  The Russian Bear when growling in his den ;
To him our Railway owes some gratitude
  And Whitwell, Wilson, hearty Kendal men.

What groups of gazers stand upon the hills
  Descending and ascending all the day ;
Each stare and muse—curiosity is strong,
  Reluctantly at last depart away.

It makes one dizzy just to take a glance
  The poor Moor-Game fly away affrighted ;
And a blithe Squirrel up in yonder tree
  He's springing from twig to twig delighted.

A sleepy Owl disturbed in his dreams
  Makes the Vale echo with his shrill wailing ;
And further down as if in dread alarm
  Rats across the Beelah now are sailing.

Some Magpies in deep consultation
  In close proximity they chatter ;
No doubt sore puzzled with the awful noise
  Discussing o'er the curious matter.

Tis like a Dream this Iron Monster Bridge
  As if rais'd up by a Magician's will ;
Or freak of Witchcraft in the Days of Old—
  A Thousand Feet across from hill to hill !

Tis done, no matter for the How or Why
  Tho' one from Kendal felt his heart grow weak ;
Could not complete the task, and lays the blame—
  On Thieves—to ease his heart when like to break.

Gilk and Wilson,—these men with honor crown
  They merit all our hearty honest praise ;
This noble work hath gain'd them high renown
  Enough to gild with Glory all their days,

Napoleon fought for Kingdoms—these for Fame,
  And for their Country's good incessant toil ;
A Conquest o'er stupendous Hills and Stones
  They spread the Rails, in spite of swampy soil !

O'er Vallies—Planes—they stretch amazing far,
  Each brook and streamlet murm'ring down below ;
Nought stops their progress till the work is done
  And then what thousands travel to and fro.

Beelah, no more shall Solitude enthrall
  Or Silence reign supreme on all around ;
The spell is broke, a thousand hearts rejoice
  Survey the Sight with wonder how profound.

And Troy, of which old Homer sweetly sings
  The Wooden Horse and how they battl'd then ;
The Ancients never dreamt of such a thing
  To fly by Steam in spite of wind or rain.

Egypt, thy Spinxes, Pyramids and Tombs
  Rear'd up to please thy Monarchs silly pride ;
Stupendous Monuments of Toil and Death
  With dusty Mummies sleeping side by side.

Bab'lon, thy Hanging Gardens—Gates of Brass
  And Golden Image set on Dura's plane ;
No doubt were wondrous in that gloomy age
  Daniel knew such gods were weak and vain.

Athens, with all thy Learning—Statues grand—
  And Classic Sculpture, voluptuous forms
Our Bridge like a Colossus spans the Vale
  And may it stand a thousand winter's storms.

Rome, tell us not of all thy pomp and glory
  Thy Marble Columns and thy Towers tall ;
For Beelah 'mid her Dells and swampy waste
  Her IRON WONDER far surpasses all.

Great Clifford's Son who with some Shepherds dwelt
  On Stainmore Forest as Old Records tell ;
Ne'er dreamt of such a wondrous sight as this
  While musing lonely by the Dropping Well.

Old Baxter, he surnam'd the " Wise-Man" great
  Who Rais'd the Devil—so the old folks say—
Were he to come again no doubt would stare
  And wonder where we found the cash to pay.

All hail to Steam ! all hail to Men of Brains
  Who sweep away all obstacles before them ;
Cut down our Hills and through the Mountains bore
  And make admiring crowds adore them.

And while upon Old Stainmore's Hills we stand
  And muse what Men of Mind so well can do ;
Say—when we've paid them with our Gold
  Shall we not give them Praise and Honor too ?

' The cloud cap'd Towers, the solemn Temples"—
  [As Shakespear tells us in his Verse sublime] ;
Our Iron Bridge dissolve and pass away
  When there shall also be an end of Time.

Nay "the great Globe itself" he plainly says—
  Shall disappear and then be seen no more ;
We don't believe this creed—our world will still—
  Move round the Sun as she has done before.

But when "the Archangel's Trump shall sound"
  As good John Wesley piously he sings ;
May we among the heav'nly host be found
  When we have bid farewell to earthly things.

* Note.—We are glad to give the Right Hand of Fellowship to the Sons of Genius where ever and whenever we chance to meet. All admirers of sterling Genius will be pleased to hear that Mr Robson, Author of those graphic and exquisite Sketches called " Black Comb, and "A Lake Tour in the Whitehaven District, is come to dwell among us while searching for Iron Stone ; we hope he will succeed. [J. C

Poet's Hall, Kirkby-Stephen, Sept. 17th, 1859.

Kirkby-Stephen, Printed & Sold by J. Close, (One Penny.

A ballad by J. Close of Poet's Hall, Kirkby Stephen, in praise of Thomas Bouch and his viaduct. These literary masterpieces were sold around the markets of the area.

A superb view of the Belah Viaduct with a double-headed passenger train. For many years this practice was not permitted and a banking engine was usually needed. The LNER relaxed the weight restrictions almost entirely in later years.

Believed to be the first use of a locomotive with a leading bogie in the UK, this was one of six commissioned by William Bouch for use on the Stainmore gradients. Built by Robert Stephenson & Co. of Newcastle, it closely resembles those built for the Grand Trunk Railway of Canada. The generous cabs on the first two were derided by hardier drivers and removed.

The South Durham & Lancashire Union Railway

Various schemes were mooted for linking the railways east and west of the Pennines. The Newcastle & Carlisle was the first to be built on the easiest route, but a crossing further south was needed. The post of engineer was offered to Thomas Bouch in January 1856 on the basis of £50 per mile for preparing the Bill and survey drawings and for 'fighting' it through Parliament. Clearly Bouch was anticipating opposition, but things moved fast and the Bill was deposited at Westminster in time for the 1857 session. The Act was obtained on 13 July 1857, and all work in preparing plans and supervision up to the time of opening was undertaken by Bouch for a fee of £150 per mile.

This was still very 'economical' for a line with major engineering works and through difficult country, to be built to main line standards, although a single line would be laid initially. For some unexplained reason the Directors decided that three of the masonry viaducts should be built for single line only.

The first sod was cut at Kirkby Stephen by none other than the Duke of Cleveland himself on 25 August 1857. The work went ahead, though never fast enough to please the Directors, and there were problems with the labour force, and four police constables, paid by the Company, were recommended to keep the peace. The Directors were only willing to pay for one unfortunate man. By July 1861 the 34¾ miles were ready for inspection by the Board of Trade. It was a considerable tribute to Bouch's management that the line was approved at the first inspection, and it was opened to passenger traffic on 8 August 1861.

The Stainmore line was well known, not only for penetrating some of the wildest country south of the Scottish Border, but also for its remarkable iron trestle viaducts at Belah and Deepdale, and a slightly smaller one across the Tees just west of Barnard Castle, originally built for a single line and having stone piers. The reason for using iron trestles was the need for speed of construction, and the height. Material excavated on the east side was urgently needed for embankments on the west side of these two deep valleys, and without it construction would have been unacceptably delayed while waiting for the masonry to harden. In terms of cost there was little to choose between them. Deepdale had eleven clear spans of 60ft each, and a maximum height of 161ft. Belah was somewhat larger with sixteen similar spans and a maximum height of 196ft.

Bouch had no previous experience of large iron bridges, since all the bridges between Lancaster and Carlisle had been of timber. The design of the trestles was not so critical as that of the girders since the main loading was vertical, but the girders had to take a distributed load over each span of 60 tons, or 240 tons central breaking load, so that a pair of girders, one under each rail, would carry 60 tons or 1 ton per foot run which was the norm at that time. Bouch sought the help of Robert Henry Bow of Edinburgh, who had published in 1850 a comprehensive treatise on braced structures which became a classic. Bow described himself as a civil engineer, and is recorded as having spent one session at Edinburgh University studying mathematics, but he developed an expertise in graphical statistics, which was later praised by the eminent scientist, James Scott-Maxwell. He also devised Bow's Notation, known to many a schoolboy. He favoured a form of lattice girder where the diagonals were in pairs which crossed at right angles. There were no intermediate vertical members.

Bouch was persuaded of the virtues of this construction, which offered a maximum economy of material and became very fashionable in the UK until the end of the nineteenth century. As for the trestles, it is likely that these were designed by Gilkes, Wilson & Co. of Middlesbrough, who may have tendered on a design and build basis. Whatever the circumstances, they did a very professional job and made Bouch's name, as well as their own, known throughout the civil engineering profession. The concept was not original, and owed much to the famous Crumlin Viaduct, built by T.W. Kennard in South Wales and opened in 1857. Kennard boldly used Warren girders of 150ft span, but Bouch was feeling his way, as was Bow, and was content with 60ft girders, and correspondingly lighter trestles.

On a passing note, despite the apparent frailty of the Belah and Deepdale viaducts, in 1947 the LNER withdrew all weight restrictions, allowing the heaviest engines to cross providing that the two heaviest classes did not exceed 30mph. Although the LNER had planned some strengthening it was never carried out. It is reported that at least once the Darlington breakdown crane had crossed on its way to Kirkby Stephen. The crane weighed 156 tons, and three empty trucks were placed between the engine and the crane. Only the engine crew was allowed to stay onboard during the crossing. This was a great tribute to the work of Bouch and his associates who had built better than they knew.

The Tees Viaduct west of Barnard Castle had five spans of 120ft each, on stone piers up to 132ft high. This seems to have gone out to tender, probably because Gilkes, Wilson already had their hands full. T.W. Kennard, of the Viaduct Works, Crumlin, was awarded the contract, but used the X form of bracing which may have been specified by Bouch.

The branch from Barnard Castle to Bishop Auckland did not open until 1 August 1863, for a dispute arose with the Duke of Cleveland who required the line to be diverted. This line was included in the original Act of 1857 and would have been laid out by Bouch. It ran north-east from Barnard Castle for about 11 miles, where it joined the long-established Haggerleases branch in the valley of the Gaunless at Spring Gardens. There was an iron viaduct on stone piers, the Lands Viaduct, with four spans of 120ft and a maximum height of 93ft closely resembling the Tees Viaduct and these girders too may have come from Crumlin. This was needed to cross the valley of the Gaunless, and there were two large stone viaducts before the branch reached Tees Valley Junction and Barnard Castle.

At Stainmore summit the main line rose to 1,370ft above sea level, and there were long stretches around 1:60 either side of the summit. Stainmore Summit was the third highest in England. Between Bowes and Barras, for over 10 miles, there was no intermediate station, which offers some indication of the desolation. Bouch's early optimism, as conveyed to John Dixon, quickly evaporated, but taking into account the lie of the land, his sweeping curves showed that he had mastered the art of laying out a main line railway under difficult conditions, and without resorting to tunnelling. Joseph Locke would have approved. Such an opportunity was unlikely to arise again, for by 1860 most of the trunk lines were already in existence.

West of Barnard Castle there were six major stone viaducts, with fifty-three arches of 30ft each in total. The largest was at Smardale with fourteen arches up to 90ft high, near to where the Stainmore line joined the LNWR Lancaster & Carlisle line at a south-facing junction. This allowed trains to run direct towards the Furness industrial area, but this was a very roundabout route to Whitehaven and Workington where the ironworks were also developing rapidly.

The Eden Valley Railway and the Cockermouth, Keswick & Penrith

Even when the SD&LUR plans were first under discussion, it was realised that a branch from Kirkby Stephen northwards towards what became Clifton Junction on the LNWR, a distance of 22 miles, and from there another 4¼ miles to Penrith, was highly desirable. The Cockermouth, Keswick & Penrith Railway could then be joined at Penrith, and from Cockermouth there already existed a line to Workington opened on 28 April 1847 after inspection by the formidable Captain Simmons RE. It was January 1865 before the line to Keswick and Penrith opened.

Podgill Viaduct on the Stainmore railway was one of three built initially for only a single line, which soon proved to be a false economy. A second identical structure was built later, but the difference in the stone used is just discernible.

Above: Smardale Viaduct on the Stainmore line between Kirkby Stephen and Tebay. Although built for a double line, the volume of traffic never justified doubling and it remained a single line. Most of the mineral traffic went up the Eden Valley line to Penrith.

Opposite top: The Crozier Holme Bridge after very substantial strengthening, which included the insertion of heavy beams beneath each line of rails. While the CKPR remained an independent company until 1923, it had always resisted pressure from the LNWR for this to be done.

Opposite middle: This little drawing is of interest because it is one of the very few surviving carrying Bouch's signature. The bridge in question is what looks like an accommodation bridge on the Cockermouth, Keswick & Penrith Railway but where is not known.

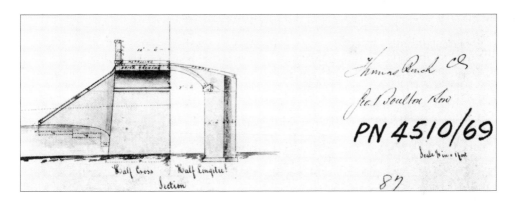

An inverted bowstring girder at Rowsome on the CKPR after massive strengthening. Where clearance under the girder allowed, this permitted sway bracing, as visible on the Crozier Holme Bridge, to be hidden inside the girder.

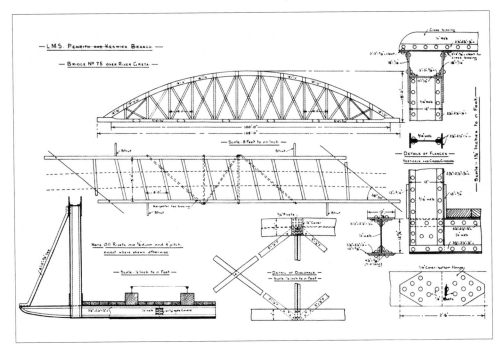

A drawing from the LMS Bridge Office at Euston showing the 101ft span of the Crozier Holme Bridge over the river Greta east of Keswick as built. Much strengthening was carried out to allow Royal Scot locomotives on tourist trains to reach Keswick.

The original Lands or Cockfield Viaduct crossing the older lines in the Gaunless Valley. This was on the extension of the Stainmore line from Barnard Castle to serve North Durham. It was rebuilt for a double line on the same piers by the NER.

A closer view of Hownes Gill Viaduct shortly after it was first completed. Scaffolding has been erected to add extra buttresses to the base of the piers to increase lateral stability. This was done on the advice of Robert Stephenson.

Hownes Gill Viaduct opened in 1858, but this view is some years later after tree growth started to hide its impressive height. Its remarkably slim arches, built in fire brick, are a tribute to both Thomas Bouch and his contractor.

The Eden Valley Railway

The Eden Valley Railway Act received the Royal Assent on 21 May 1858, once again with Thomas Bouch as engineer, and a fortnight later the first sod was cut by Lord Brougham and Vaux. The single line with passing places opened for passenger traffic on 9 June 1862. For some unknown reason the Eden Valley was planned to join the LNWR with a south facing connection at Clifton Junction, and a further Act was needed in 1862 to correct this error, but for over a year all trains from the EVR to Penrith had to reverse at Clifton. Since another reversal was required at Penrith to reach the Cockermouth line, there would have been considerable delays in working had the Cockermouth line been open. When in 1863 the Eden Valley became part of the North Eastern Railway, a third Act allowed a cut-off curve to be built, avoiding Penrith for through trains to Cockermouth after the opening of that line in 1865.

There were no heavy engineering works on the EVR. Two viaducts at Musgrave and Skygarth had lattice girders on stone piers, while the stone viaduct at Copeland had five arches of 30ft. The Musgrave viaduct had three spans of 63ft, and at Skygarth there were four spans of 98ft. Elsewhere cast-iron humpback girders were used, and, as might have been expected with Bouch as engineer, all iron bridging material was supplied by Gilkes, Wilson & Co. of Middlesbrough. The cost of building the line was modest at under £10,000 a mile, but though being mostly single line it was designed to carry heavy mineral traffic and was in no way a rural 'light railway'.

The Cockermouth, Keswick & Penrith Railway

Together with the existing Cockermouth & Workington Railway, the CK&PR formed the final link in the east/west route between the industrial areas of Durham and West Cumberland. The Act was granted on 1 August 1861, and the first sod was cut by Mr Hoskins, Chairman of the Company, in May 1862. It was a local company unconnected with the Stockton & Darlington, but Bouch was appointed as engineer. Although it passed through some very difficult country east of Keswich, the line was opened throughout on 2 January 1865. Unlike the Darlington to Penrith lines, which became part of the North Eastern Railway in 1863, the CK&PR remained independent until 1923 when it became part of the LMS.

There was considerable stone traffic from local quarries along the route in addition to the heavy traffic of coke and iron ore. Passing as it did through the northern part of the Lake District, it was described by some as the most scenic line in England, and over the course of time heavy tourist traffic developed. At Keswick a large hotel was built by private interests, and was connected to the station by a covered way.

The summit was at Troutback where the line rose to 889ft (only 26ft less than the notorious Shap Fell), but the most difficult part was the 4 miles from Thelkeld into Keswick through the thickly wooded gorge of the Greta, which the line had to cross eight times on bowstring girder bridges.

Beyond Keswick the going was much easier, though there was a stretch of marshy, sometimes flooded, ground where the Derwent was crossed. It was here that Bouch used screw piles instead of driven timber piles, perhaps for the first time. They were of cast iron, a foot in diameter, with a very coarse external screw thread, made in sections, and could be screwed into soft ground until friction would not allow further rotation. Some years later, when used on the South Esk Bridge at Montrose, they were shown to be much more reliable than conventional piling. Along the south side of Bassenthwaite Lake the line was mostly level, with a rise of 1:100 for 1½ miles before dropping down into the valley of the Cocker, and making a head on connection to the C&WR at Cockermouth.

The CK&PR was notable for the large number of bridges required and both cast-iron girders and the much larger trussed bowstring girders were the work of Gilkes, Wilson & Co. of Middlesbrough, who also supplied a cast-iron arch bridge to cross the Greta on the approach road to the station and hotel at Keswick. There were two stone viaducts, the one at Mosedale having twelve spans of 30ft, and the Penruddock Viaduct had nine spans of about 25ft.

The choice of bowstring trusses was new for Bouch, and may well have been suggested by Robert Bow as the most suitable for crossing from side to side of a deep gorge in one span. The only other bridge of this type used by Bouch was at Auchendinny on the Penicuik line where conditions were very similar. Such girders needed overhead sway bracing or outriggers at the side, and where the clearance over the river allowed, Bouch used inverted girders braced from below. There were three of these and four upright girders, with spans between 80 and 119ft.

The CK&PR had been built to the standards of its time for a secondary main line, as had the lines to the east, and train weights and locomotive workings were restricted to 0-6-0 tender engines, with another banker at the rear on the Stainmore section. On the CK&PR locomotives and crews were provided by the LNWR. Having introduced 0-8-0 engines, the LNWR expressed a wish to use these to allow heavier mineral trains. The CK&PR management offered no objection if the LNWR paid for the essential strengthening of bridges. The LNWR refused since the bridges were the property of the CK&PR. The latter refused to spend money for the benefit of the LNWR, and so for many years the situation remained. It was only when the line became part of the LMS in 1923 that extensive strengthening was done, with the result that by 1939 engines of the 'Black 5' 4-6-0 type could work through to Keswick where a turntable had been installed, and on occasion in summer when traffic was very heavy, 'Royal Scot's' would put in an appearance at Keswick.

While in his early years as a consultant Bouch had sometimes behaved in an unbusinesslike way, to say the least, he retrieved his reputation on these north country lines. He was now over forty years of age and had clearly matured. Even greater things lay ahead back in Scotland.

Hownes Gill Viaduct

Thomas Bouch was responsible for a large number of brick or masonry viaducts from Montrose in the north down to Eynsford in Kent, on the line between Swanley Junction and Sevenoaks. The graceful viaduct across Hownes Gill, near Consett in Durham, is architecturally one of his finest.

The line over the viaduct had been built as part of the Stanhope & Tyne Railway, which nearly bankrupted its engineer, Robert Stephenson. It opened on 15 May 1834, and was planned to carry limestone from a new quarry high in the Pennines at Stanhope down to the sea at South Shields. Several rope-worked inclines were required but at Hownes Gill there was what can only be described as a ravine, 800ft wide and 160ft deep.

Rails laid to a gauge of 7ft were installed down one side of the valley on a gradient of 1:2½ and up the other side at 1:3. A 20hp steam engine at the bottom operated both inclines simultaneously. It was a difficult and potentially dangerous device, and could only handle twelve wagons an hour. Proposals for a bridge were put forward in 1836 and again in 1844 but nothing was done, and for twenty-four years this bottleneck existed, although improvements in 1853 increased the capacity to thirty-six wagons hourly.

When the S&T was taken over by the Stockton & Darlington in 1863, Bouch was invited by John Dixon, engineer of the S&D, to build a viaduct at Hownes Gill, and in 1856 plans were prepared for a viaduct of twelve semicircular arches of 50ft span, and rising to 150ft. It is thought that the contractor and master mason, John Anderson, had assisted with the design which was unusually slim, and the Directors were wary and thought it best to consult Robert Stephenson. He reported that while the design was basically sound, he would advise the use of inverts between the arches to reduce the ground pressure, and to extend the bases of the highest piers to give greater lateral stability in high winds. In earlier times shallow mining had taken place in the area and the position of some of the old workings was unknown, while others were still accessible.

An unusual feature of the viaduct was the material used. No suitable building stone existed in the neighbourhood, and such bricks as were available nearby were of inferior quality. The nearest source of good bricks was at Crook, where Pease's Wear Firebrick Co., part of the Pease family's industrial empire, could supply firebricks of excellent quality. Over 2½ million of these were used. Their suitability has been well proven, for the viaduct has endured the Pennine weather for 150 years.

A slight mystery exists, as all photographs show ten arches, and all the written descriptions speak of twelve of 50ft span. Since on this occasion the camera cannot lie it is conceivable that there was a last minute design change to ten arches of 60ft. The reason may have been because of bad ground conditions.

Although the viaduct has not carried a train for many years, it continues to serve the public as a footpath.

Locomotives for Stainmore

The gradients over Stainmore involved a long slog in either direction even in the best of conditions, and in winter snow often led to complete blockages. The longest was during the winter of 1947 when the line either side of Barras was blocked from 3 February until the end of March. The Stockton & Darlington lacked suitable locomotive power, and since double-heading over the iron viaducts was forbidden, it became the custom to use a banking engine at the rear at the suggestion of William Bouch, the Locomotive Superintendent. When the question of introducing a new type of heavier locomotive arose, William considered that the use of a leading bogie might be advantageous. At that time the vast majority of British locomotives had rigid frames, but the South Devon and the North London lines used 4-4-0 tank engines. William visited these, and was impressed by their riding qualities, and he recommended the purchase of 4-4-0 tender locomotives to the S&D Directors.

Robert Stephenson had for long advocated the use of leading bogie locomotives, with little success at home. His works at Newcastle did, however, build a number of this type for the Grand Trunk Railway of Canada and elsewhere abroad. Tenders were invited by the S&D for two bogie engines, with an option for another four, and Robert Stephenson & Co. received the order for the first two to be delivered prior to the opening of the line early in 1860.

These were handsome and businesslike engines, and groundbreaking in that they had generous cabs of the American type, particularly well suited for the Stainmore weather in winter. Unfortunately, this unwonted luxury caused jealousy (or envy?) among the other less fortunate drivers on the S&D, and the cosseted drivers were so ridiculed that they begged for the cabs to be removed. The remaining four engines were delivered with only the customary weatherboards.

8

SCHEMES TO CROSS THE FORTH AND A STRANGE BRIDGE OVER THE TYNE

The cost and inconvenience to the EP&D and its successor, the NBR, involved in transporting goods and passengers across the Firth of Forth between Granton and Burntisland was a constant drain on the resources of the companies. Although there seems to be no record of a railway passenger, let alone a ferry, being lost in stormy weather, wise passengers for Dundee found the Caledonian route, through Stirling and Perth, more comfortable and taking no longer. To some extent Thomas Bouch with his wagon ferries had greatly improved the transit of goods, but the Directors of the NBR were not blind to their inability to offer an attractive passenger service avoiding ferries or change of train. Early in the 1860s the Chairman, Richard Hodgson, instructed Bouch to devise a workable scheme for a bridge over the Forth.

The favoured site was in the vicinity of Queensferry, where the firth narrowed to under a mile and Inchgarvie Island offered a rock foundation for a pier in mid-channel. Even so two spans of at least 1,600ft each were unavoidable. The great Thomas Telford, after problems with high winds damaging his suspension bridge at Menai, considered an 800ft span to be the absolute limit. When supplies of wrought iron became more generally available at the beginning of the nineteenth century, a young Edinburgh land surveyor, James Anderson, prepared a detailed but impracticable scheme for a suspension bridge. With the technology of the time he could not hope to attain the minimum span necessary, and there could be no question of founding intermediate piers in the deep water channels either side of Inchgarvie, which are up to 240ft in depth. For the same reason proposals for tunnels proved to be out of the question.

Bouch dismissed the idea of a suspension bridge for railway use since Captain Samuel Brown's bridge over the Tees had failed to cope with quite a small rolling load. It would have to be a lattice girder bridge or nothing, but certainly not at Queensferry. Two eminent engineering consultants, George Robert Stephenson, cousin of the more famous Robert, and John Furness Tone, were engaged by the NBR to make recommendations for a more suitable site, and came down in favour of a crossing further upstream, where a spur of rock called Blackness Point projected into the channel opposite the small harbour at Charlestown on the north shore. There was an existing railway, hardly more than a tramway, from beyond Dunfermline to Charlestown, which brought down coal from pits up country to the little harbour. Part of the route could be incorporated in the new line, but only after complete rebuilding.

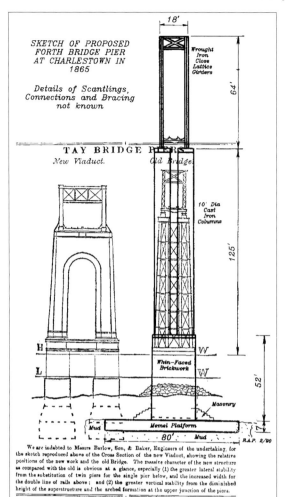

Sketches originally showing a comparison between the piers of the first and second Tay bridges. Superimposed is an outline of one of the proposed piers for Bouch's first scheme to bridge the Forth between Charlestown and Blackness Point.

South of the river, the proposal was to build a new line along the shore from Granton Harbour. Apart from bridging the Avon at Cramond it was an easy run, though it involved passing through the policies of Dalmeny House, seat of Lord Rosebery, from whom some opposition might be expected when the Bill came before the House of Lords. The most implacable opposition came from up-river ports like Grangemouth, Alloa and the Scottish Central Railway since the Forth carried far more commercial traffic than the Tay. Their concern was that the piers of the bridge would obstruct the navigation channel or cause silting which would involve periodic dredging. Bouch had originally conceived spans of 600ft, but was persuaded by the company to reduce this to four spans of 500ft each. This would not satisfy the opposition until it was pointed out to them that the whole trade of the Port of London was carried out over a channel barely 500ft wide in places.

The bridge was to allow a clearance for the masts of the largest sailing ships using the river, and the minds of the Commons Committee were much exercised as to how Bouch proposed to found his massive masonry piers in the glacial silt which filled the deep channel scoured in the rock by the glaciers of the last Ice Age. Bouch had employed Jesse Wylie, an experienced mineral borer, to find a hard bottom, but in one place a sounding of 231ft failed to reach it. The series of borings was very extensive across the whole width of the river and samples of the materials were sent to Stevenson Macadam, chemist, at an analytical laboratory in Edinburgh. A method of virtually floating the foundations in the consolidated mixture of silt and sand was suggested by Bouch. It may not have been an original idea but certainly had never been attempted before on such a scale. The Committee had reservations but allowed themselves to be persuaded by Bouch's supreme confidence in his proposals.

Information on the form of the girders is lacking, and the only guide is a diagrammatic drawing in the library of the Earl of Elgin showing a close lattice for the minor spans. When the girders for the Stainmore viaducts were designed by Robert H. Bow some years earlier, he had adopted what was then an unusual arrangement of diagonals with no vertical members, and this X bracing was to become popular for the next half-century. It forms a prominent feature of the present Forth Rail Bridge.

At the Tay Bridge Inquiry of 1880, Bouch stated in his evidence that he had come across this form of bracing some years before and had adopted it, and certainly used it throughout his Tay Bridge and elsewhere. This suggests that he would have adopted it in the Charlestown viaduct, but the spans of 60ft clear at Stainmore were a different proposition to the 500ft spans over the Forth, where the girders would be 64ft in height with diagonals 90ft in length. Robert Bow was a theorist and probably shied away from such an undertaking, and this may have been when Bouch first consulted Allan Duncan Stewart, a young mathematician in Edinburg of great ability.

Each pier was to be supported on a platform of green beech, 114ft x 80ft x 9ft in depth. This would limit the pressure on the silt to ¾ ton psf, a very conservative figure, but he had little to guide him. The beech, being slightly heavier than water, would not float. A wrought-iron cylinder of about 30ft diameter would rest on the platform and be filled with masonry, with an outer covering of whinstone. As the platform sank under the weight the column would be built up until the platform ceased to sink and the top of the cylinder was 12ft above high water. A pair of 10ft-diameter cast-iron cylinders would then be carried up to the height of the girders. This was all very well but Bouch determined to build a trial pier before committing the company too far.

Shortly after the Bill was submitted to Parliament, a trial was made using two wrought-iron cylinders 60ft high and 6ft in diameter, which were erected vertically on the river bed. One cylinder was open at the bottom and the other closed. The sinking of the cylinder was started on Sunday, 6 November 1864 but Bouch was not present. The first cylinder fell over with 60 tons on top but there was success with the second. The foreman, John Anderson, reported to Bouch by letter that at low tide there was a weight of 80 tons on the cylinder and it had sunk $1^5/8$ ins. He had another 40 tons of iron on hand and had sent to Bo'ness for more. There is no report of how the experiment ended, but Bouch was sufficiently satisfied with the bearing capacity of the silt to proceed with his scheme after the passing of the Act.

Up until the early 1860s the NBR had expanded greatly, with its proposals for a £5 million trunk line to Carlisle – best known when opened in 1862 as the Waverley Line – opened on 1 November 1849 as far as Hawick, only to prove a white elephant for lack of traffic. In addition there had been considerable capital outlay in taking over a number of small branch lines, and earlier amalgamation with the Edinburgh & Glasgow and the takeover of the Edinburgh, Perth & Dundee on 1 August 1862. All this had been achieved by the driving force and ambition of the NBR Chairman, Richard Hodgson. The effect of this empire building, much of it aimed at frustrating the Caledonian, was that the NBR became impoverished, and would have been unable to pay a dividend in the latter half of 1866. Moreover, the auditors had been tipped off by a whistleblower within the company that the Secretary, J.P. Lythgoe, had been cooking the books on orders from Hodgson, and that previous dividends had been paid out of capital, a deadly sin. The investigation which followed reported that the company needed £1 million immediately to keep it on an even keel and that officers of the company were involved in various malpractices for their own benefit. Hodgson fought his corner tenaciously but was forced to resign on 13 November 1866, under a threat of prosecution.

The Redheugh road bridge between Newcastle and Gateshead over the deep valley of the Tyne. One of the 27in-diameter tubes forming the compression members of the girders is visible on the left. These were designed to carry gas. The pipes on the right were 12in water mains carried on the bottom booms.

The Redheugh bridge showing the girders with a footpath cantilevered out each side. The girders were continuous for increased strength, anchored at the centre pier with expansion joints at the abutments.

In June 1866 Bouch had been instructed to proceed with a full-sized trial pier. This had a platform of Memel pine, which was then widely available in large sizes and much used in construction work but, unlike green beech, it floated freely. The platform was 80ft x 60ft x 7ft in depth and was towed up from Burntisland and anchored in position. Masons and bricklayers were engaged to build up the central pillar some 30ft in diameter. After it had sunk to the river bed, it was intended to load it temporarily with 10,000 tons of iron in order to settle the platform firmly into the silt. On 3 August 1866, when only preliminary work had been done on sinking the platform, the unexpected arrival of Richard Hodgson and several other Directors brought the news that all work was to cease immediately and the men to be paid-off. The timber in the platform had considerable salvage value, and orders were given for it to be towed back to Burntisland for disposal, while the iron tube ended up as scrap at Middlesbrough. In all, the development had cost the NBR £34,390 with nothing to show for it. After the Tay Bridge Inquiry, a critic, seeking a stick with which to beat the unfortunate engineer, most unfairly held this loss against Bouch, who had only done what was expected of him.

A customer was soon found for the timber platform. Richard Cail, one of the trustees of the Redheugh Bridge at Newcastle, of which Bouch was the engineer, had it towed to the Tyne where it supplied all the necessary scaffolding and decking, and was sold off for a useful sum after completion of the bridge.

Thomas Bouch had other schemes in mind but Victorian finance suffered one of its periodical crises in 1866 culminating in the failure of the bank of Overend & Gurney in Norwich. Since most of the capital of the NBR had been provided by shareholders in England, even in more propitious times it would have struggled to drag itself out of the financial morass into which Hodgson had plunged it. For the time being there were to be no more big bridges. The start of the long drawn-out saga of the Tay Bridge was still several years away.

The Remarkable Bridge at Redheugh

A year or so earlier, the Bill for Bouch's only major road bridge, at Redheugh, linking Newcastle with Gateshead, had gone before Parliament, and the Act was passed in 1867. The purpose of the bridge was to allow development of a large area of good building land lying to the west of Gateshead, and only accessible by a steep descent into the Tyne Valley and an equally steep climb out again. The new bridge would be approached by several conventional masonry arches from each bank. It was the ironwork of the bridge that exhibited unusual features. The two main girders were to have Bouch's favourite X bracing and to be formed in one continuous length of 743ft. The lower U-shaped tension flanges were to be 27in wide, with each accommodating a 12in water main. The top compression members followed the practice of I.K. Brunel in having a tubular form of 27' diameter, but the remarkable feature was that these would serve also as gas mains. A pair of lattice towers 64ft high above each pier carried tension bars 15in x ¾in which supported the deck at one third span. The road deck was 20ft wide, with 7ft walkways cantilevered out on each side. This was designed to accommodate horse-drawn traffic only, with no concentrated rolling loads. By the end of the century the growth in traffic necessitated a new bridge which could also take steam rollers and road locomotives weighing up to 20 tons.

The four 12ft diameter caissons supporting each of the three river piers were sunk under compressed air to 60ft below high water as required by the Tyne Commission, and filled with concrete. On each of these, four 3ft-diameter cast-iron columns, firmly braced together, were carried up to girder height. There was no main contractor, the Bridge Trustees apparently sub-contracting portions of the work under the close supervision of their Chairman, Richard Cail, himself a civil engineer. Being a Bouch concept, the Redheugh Bridge displayed some unusual features, and Bouch himself described it as a stiffened suspension bridge, a principle which he hoped to incorporate in his second attempt at a Forth Bridge, but this time at Queensferry. Comparing the two designs, it is difficult to distinguish common characteristics except that the aim was to keep the deck as rigid as possible under concentrated rolling loads.

A Second Attempt at Crossing the Forth

The detailed design of the second Forth Bridge was started in about 1872 when the Tay Bridge was at last underway. The Act for the new connecting lines and the bridge itself was passed on 5 August 1873, with the proviso that work on the bridge must be started by 30 September 1878. This proved to be a very close-run thing as the bridge was to be built on behalf of a consortium of four companies. The North British was in no position to put up its share of the costs being fully committed on the Tay Bridge, and the other three companies, the North Eastern, the Midland and the Great Northern, were not prepared to start until the North British, which was the one that stood to gain the greatest benefit from the bridge, could come up with the money. For four years there was an impasse which allowed Bouch breathing space to refine his design.

There were misgivings in various quarters about the design of the structure, for nothing like it had ever been seen before. The three main towers were to be 550ft in height and the spans between them to be an unheard of 1,600ft. The centre towers, spaced 120ft apart to assist lateral stability, would be built on Inchgarvie Island, and all three would have their foundations on solid rock. The supporting chains would have to carry a tensile load of 5,224 tons due to the deadweight of the bridge alone. Wrought-iron chains as used previously could only be loaded safely to 5tsi and high-tensile steel was the only alternative material. In 1873 steel was still regarded by bridge builders with suspicion, and the Board of Trade refused to accept it for railway bridges. Bessemer steel had been tried in Belgium and found unsatisfactory, being reported to be little if any stronger than cast iron. While it must be pure speculation, as no evidence is forthcoming, it seems likely that Bouch, along with other progressive engineers, lobbied the Board of Trade to permit the general use of steel, for his bridge depended on it.

A Committee consisting of Sir John Hawkshaw, W.H. Barlow and Colonel Yolland RE was set up by the Board of Trade to study the suitability of steel for structural use, and in due course they reported back favourably, but strictly subject to certain provisos to ensure consistency of quality, which was where the Belgian Bessemer steel had been found wanting. The introduction of the Siemens open hearth process in Germany in 1861 had produced steel of superior quality. This advice was accepted and in 1877 the Board of Trade notified their approval of the use of steel in new railway bridges. It was the use of steel throughout Fowler and Baker's Forth Bridge of 1890 that finally made steel acceptable to even the most conservative engineers, and sounded the knell for the large-scale production of wrought iron. But it came too late for Thomas Bouch.

The North British Directors had come to know and respect their consulting engineer, with many he was on terms of personal friendship, but his design for the Queensferry Bridge was so far ahead of its time that they referred it to William Pole and William Henry Barlow for a structural assessment. Pole was both an experienced engineer and a mathematician whose ability could not be matched outside academia. W.H. Barlow was one of the most senior men in the civil engineering profession. Both were Fellows of the Royal Society. A further Act of Parliament would have to be obtained to cover the final detailed design of the bridge, and a favourable report from such eminent engineers would carry great weight with both the Parliamentary Committee and the Board of Trade.

A full view of the Redheugh Bridge, looking down river, with the High Level Bridge and the Swing Bridge in the distance. What the railway builders left of the castle can be seen just to the right of the middle pier. The waters of the Tyne look very polluted.

The only part of Bouch's Queensferry Bridge ever to be built enabled the foundation stone to be laid within a few hours of the time limit imposed by Parliament. These pathetic remains still continue to serve a useful purpose.

Bouch's principal aim was to provide as rigid a platform as possible, so that there was a minimum of flexing as a train moved along the deck. This had been attempted with a limited degree of success by Roebling in 1855 with his 821ft-span bridge at Niagara Falls. This lasted for forty-two years but trains were always limited to 3mph. How far Bouch would have achieved his purpose was never put to the test but he envisaged it would be capable of taking trains at 'normal' speeds, maybe as much as 30mph. Barlow and Pole were clearly daunted by the scale of the problem and wrote in their report:

> We feel that the design of such a structure involves heavy responsibilities, chiefly, of course, upon the engineer of the bridge, but secondarily on all those who may concur in recommending its adoption; and we conceive that all possible means should be employed to ascertain, by the most thorough and searching enquiry, that the principles of the design are sound, and that such dimensions have been given to the parts as will be ample to ensure stability.

They set about their enquiries with the assistance of Allan Duncan Stewart, a mathematician rather than a practical bridge engineer, who for some years had worked for Bouch as his structural consultant. There were several departures from accepted practice. Firstly, the proposed droop of the chains was to be almost a quarter of the span, as compared with the maximum of one-tenth found in existing suspension bridges.

It was this that caused the need for such high towers, but the payoff was that the maximum tension and hence the size and weight of the chains could be much reduced. Here the strength of steel was essential if the bridge was to carry rather more than its own deadweight. To increase the stiffness of the deck girders, Bouch proposed the use of tie rods taken back to the point where the decks passed through the towers, as shown in the illustration.

While this had been tried at Niagara with limited success, Professor Macquorn Rankine had investigated the problem mathematically in 1858 and considered such an approach as perfectly practicable. Similarly the Astronomer Royal, Sir George Airy, had investigated the same problem in 1867 and reached a similar conclusion. Also in 1858, R.M. Ordish (who was credited by W.H. Barlow with the design of the roof at St Pancras Station) took out a patent for a similar system. Thus Stewart and Bouch had theory to support them in their venture into the unknown.

The effects of wind pressure considerably exercised the minds of the two engineers and they wrote to Sir George Airy, Astronomer Royal, for his advice, based on the extensive meteorological records held at the Greenwich Observatory. His considered reply was as follows:

> We know that upon very limited surface(s), and for very limited times, the pressure of the wind does amount sometimes to 40psf, or in Scotland probably to more. ... I think we may say that the greatest wind pressure to which a plane surface like that of the bridge will be subjected in its whole extent is 10psf.

Barlow and Pole stated:

> We entirely concur in this opinion, which we consider highly authoritative and valuable; and we may therefore safely adopt 10psf as the side pressure due to the wind.

On this advice it is probably just as well that the bridge was never built. When a few years later Benjamin Baker, with Allan Stewart as his Chief Assistant, designed the present Forth Rail Bridge, he was taking no chances and worked to a wind pressure of 56psf, twice what he would have normally recommended. However, very little was then known about the effects of wind and Allan Stewart thought that he was safe working on 20psf for the Tay Bridge, which had been designed before the Astronomer Royal's opinion was received. Certainly the fall of the Tay Bridge concentrated the minds of both engineers and academics on the wind problem. Baker experimented and found that the unit pressure on a large plate was considerably higher than on a smaller one, due to the partial vacuum created behind the greater surface. This was a factor that had never been taken into account before.

Barlow and Pole then considered the effects of temperature change on the bridge, and decided that Bouch was correct in attaching the chains to the tops of the towers, which were capable of flexing slightly under chain movements. They summed up their conclusions:

> We see no reason to doubt the strength of the bridge as designed or the sufficiency of the quantities taken for the estimate of its cost. ... We are not prepared to recommend any other plan in preference, as we have not thought it our duty to undertake such a serious task as the investigation of the comparative merits of other systems. ... We merely wish it to be understood that, while we raise no objection to Mr Bouch's system, we do not commit ourselves to an opinion that it is the best possible.

Barlow and Pole also drew attention to the problems of corrosion which would be exacerbated by salt winds blowing up the Firth. Although wrought iron offered a limited resistance to rusting, the use of high-tensile steel in the chains would present a challenge with the protective coatings then available. This was hardly a ringing endorsement but the NBR was apparently satisfied and Bouch was left free to complete his design, although the use of steel was still not formally approved by the Board of Trade.

The two engineers had reported favourably, but they considered the question of wind forces carefully as they had little previous experience to guide them, and certainly not on a structure of this size. Taking the Astronomer Royal's estimate of 10psf they estimated a horizontal thrust of 225 tons on the horizontal girders. With the benefit of hindsight this could have proved disastrously low, and perhaps it was fortunate that the bridge was never built. While Bouch had planned to use high-tensile steel with a breaking stress of 40tsi for the chains, which was expensive and hard to come by; the referees calculated that, if a lower and more ductile carbon steel was used – virtually 32-ton mild steel as used today – stressed to 8tsi, there would be a saving and less problems with corrosion.

The NBR was fully committed financially by the cost of the Tay Bridge, and this allowed Bouch several years of breathing space, though under the terms of the Act of 1873 work had to start by the end of September 1878.

The Act of Parliament passed in August 1873 authorised in principle the construction of Bouch's Forth Bridge and connecting lines, but at that stage only the proposed line of the bridge was indicated on the Parliamentary plans. It would be necessary for a second Act to be passed authorising construction of the bridge when detailed design drawings became available. By this time Bouch was a familiar face around the Committee rooms of Westminster, though he was not always accorded the same degree of respect by his professional colleagues, who considered him something of a chancer.

The members of the Parliamentary Committees and their lawyers possessed only a limited grasp of structural matters, and approval of the bridge design by two such eminent engineers as Barlow and Pole carried much weight in their deliberations. Bouch himself was, as always, supremely confident, the opposition was light and no expert witnesses were called to cross-question him. With the Act passed it was now possible to go out to tender, although a source of the steel chains still had to be established.

Amending Acts were passed in 1876, 1878 and 1879. One of these covered a reduction in the minimum clearance at high tide from 150ft to 125ft, a more realistic figure. Final clearance was given by the 1879 Act, after which the bridge plans went out to tender. As with the Tay Bridge, there were difficulties in finding firms willing to tender for such a vast project, different in design to anything proposed, let alone built, up to that time. As usual the Jeremiahs prophesied disaster.

The contractor who saved the day was William Arrol of Dalmarnock Ironworks, Glasgow. The circumstances of his birth were unpropitious, and the first twenty-nine years of his life were spent in working his way up to foreman in Laidlaw's Engineering Works in Glasgow. In 1868 he took the bold decision to set up in business on his own account as a maker of girders and boilers. Despite facing ruin when a customer became insolvent, he survived and developed an hydraulic riveter which greatly increased productivity and the quality of work compared with the previous practice of hand riveting. Steam-driven riveters had been tried some twenty years earlier but had marked limitations, especially for site work.

Meeting the Deadline at Queensferrry

By the middle of 1878, with the Tay Bridge open and bringing in revenue, the NBR and its partners could consider proceeding with the Forth Bridge: the time for action had come. The 1873 Act required work on the bridge to start by the end of September 1878, and with that date rapidly approaching, and no work done on site so far, there was something of a panic to at least lay a foundation stone. A long-standing dispute with the Board of Trade over the height of the bridge delayed work until only four days before the deadline, and consequently none of the NBR Directors were free to attend the long-awaited ceremony.

The masonry contractor, John Waddell, was instructed to build a foundation pillar for one of the centre towers on Inchgarvie Island and to prepare for a low-key stone-laying ceremony, to be entrusted to Mrs Bouch, on 30 September. A branch line to South Queensferry had been opened on 1 June 1868 and was extended to the small naval base at Port Edgar ten years later. A special train was laid on to bring Thomas and Mrs Bouch, and such VIPs as were available, from Waverley, and this arrived at South Queensferry at eleven in the morning. It was only a short walk from the station down to the Hawes Pier where they embarked for the short crossing to Inchgarvie. The weather was blustery, and waves were almost breaking over the western end of the island where John Waddell had everything prepared.

The Revd Armstrong Black offered up a prayer, and a large bottle containing newspapers and other articles was placed in a recess. Mrs Bouch took up her ceremonial silver trowel, Waddell's men carefully lowered the stone into place, and after three taps with the trowel Mrs Bouch declared the stone well and truly laid. Thankfully, in view of the inclement weather, the party retreated to the shore and the more congenial atmosphere of the Hawes Inn, where John Waddell took the Chair and the jollifications commenced. As usual on such occasions speeches were made and toasts were enthusiastically drunk. In proposing Bouch's health, John Walker, General Manager of the NBR, dwelt at some length on that gentleman's experience and capabilities, and on his thirty years of service to the NBR, adding that 'he was a gentleman whom it afforded the greatest pleasure for any one to come in contact with'. This was no mere platitude, for Bouch was much respected by the NBR Directors and officials. Thomas Bouch was a man of few words on such occasions and his reply is not recorded. After many speeches there was a toast to 'The Ladies', and at half past one the party broke up and the VIPs returned to their train, leaving John Waddell to continue the festivities.

A contract was awarded to William Arrol & Co. on 2 October 1879 for the ironwork, and to John Waddell of Bathgate for the bridge approaches and masonry. It seems likely that Arrol's original tender had been submitted at an earlier date and accepted pending future clarification, which allowed him to start preparatory work on the site. Little progress was made until the summer of 1879, when Arrol acquired land at Dalmeny, South Queensferry, for workshops and an assembly yard. On the other side of the Forth he set up a brickworks at Inverkeithing. Waddell later returned to Inchgarvie and completed the foundation pillar, which still stands today carrying a navigation light. Nothing more was ever done, for no sooner had Arrol's contract been finalised than, within three months, the Tay Bridge was down, and the whole project was postponed indefinitely.

After the fall of the Tay Bridge on 28 December 1879 there was a great public outcry, and iron bridges and Bouch with them were totally discredited. In July 1880 a Forth Bridge Abandonment Bill was placed before Parliament, and Arrol's contract was terminated and compensation paid. The Bill had passed the Commons when, at a meeting of the four companies involved held at York, a decision was reached to withdraw the Bill in case there was a change of plans in the future.

At a further meeting on 30 September 1881, a scheme for a cantilever bridge was submitted to the NBR Board by John Fowler and Benjamin Baker, and was accepted after no more than two hours debate. The meeting further agreed that a Bill should be prepared in time for the 1882 Parliamentary Session. There was little opposition, and the Act received the Royal Assent on 12 July 1882, with work starting in December. William Arrol was again the successful contractor. The rest, as they say, is history.

9

THE TAY BRIDGE, 1873–1877

The story of the Tay Bridge is generally well known, though much more has been written about its fall than its planning and construction which spread over fifteen years. Frustrating years for Bouch as the local interests squabbled between themselves over the siting, and whether or not a bridge should be built at all. Thomas Thornton, of Patullo & Thornton, solicitors of Dundee, was the driving force from the beginning in 1863, though it was another year before a public meeting was called. Bouch was called on continually to revise his plans in an attempt to buy off one vested interest or another. It was a thankless task for which he received little or no remuneration, and without the steadfast support of Thornton and his business friends he might have been tempted to forego his plans, which had occupied his mind for twenty years.

The furthest outpost of the EP&D lay at Ferryport-on-Craig and it was there that Bouch had his first view of the Firth of Tay early in 1849, having endured a wintry crossing of the Forth to Burntisland on the open deck of one of the primitive steamers then in service. He was left in no doubt that if the EP&D was ever to capture the east coast traffic to Dundee and Aberdeen, the crude ferryboats had to go with the minimum of delay. The Tay ferries, running between Ferryport-on-Craig (soon to be renamed Tayport) and Broughty Ferry on the north bank, where there was a rail connection to the Dundee & Arbroath Railway, were jointly owned by the NBR and the Caledonian. Although two much larger ferries had been ordered by Thomas Grainger, still consulting engineer to the EP&D, it was obvious that these could only be a stopgap (although a remarkably successful one over the following three decades).

Bouch wasted no time in putting into service, as soon as they arrived, the large wagon ferries already ordered from Napier in Glasgow. Bouch's important contribution, on which the whole success of the wagon ferries depended, was a system of adjustable loading ramps at each ferry berth, which allowed far quicker handling than the hydraulic cranes ordered by Grainger, some of the first built by W.G. Armstrong of Elswick. This story is told elsewhere. Ferries though would remain at best a poor makeshift, and Bouch was totally convinced that, in time to come, bridges over the Forth and Tay would offer the only permanent solution, and he aimed to be the man to build them. These were still early days, and those to whom Bouch vouchsafed his ideas regarded him as a young visionary. He learned to keep his own counsel and bide his time, until in the summer of 1854 he was bold enough to offer his plans for bridging the Tay to the Directors of the Scottish North-Eastern Railway, but his ideas were quickly dismissed as impracticable.

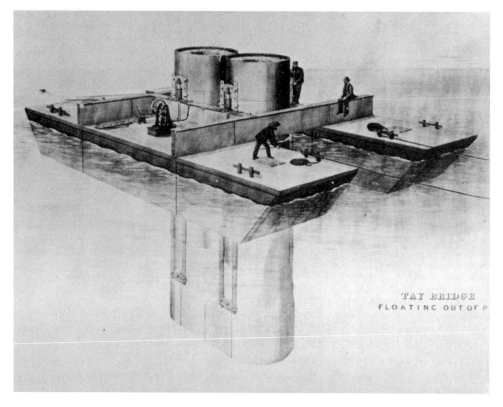

TAY BRIDGE
FLOATING OUT OF P

Floating out of the caisssons for the first brick piers on the Wormit side. Attempts to sink individual caissons in their correct positions were frustrated by wind and tides, and they had to be made in pairs as shown.

For a start, the Tay at Dundee was nearly a mile and a half wide, though with no great depth of water and much of the channel was obstructed by shifting sandbanks. The tides were fierce, and the estuary subjected to severe storms, even occasional hurricanes. What lay in the bed of the river no one knew. Had Bouch been a wiser man he would have started by consulting the geologists at Edinburgh University. As it was he came to rely on borings which proved woefully inadequate.

Several books and innumerable articles have been written on the Tay Bridge in the 125 years since its fall, but history remains indebted to Albert Groethe, Site Manager for the erection contractors, for the most comprehensive history of the early politicking, which he published in June 1878. Groethe was proud of the bridge and his part in it, and never lost an opportunity to publicise it, occasionally to the neglect of his other duties. Bouch had a hard fight over many years against conflicting interests before he could inspire the NBR to take on what was still widely regarded as a 'castle in the air', its failure inevitable. There were strong vested interests opposed, from the ferry proprietors to the harbour authorities at Dundee, Newburgh, and as far up-river as Perth, aided by the inevitable contingent of doom-mongers.

An article in the *Dundee Advertiser* of 6 November 1863 first publicly broached the idea of a bridge as being practicable and desirable. Less than a year later, in October 1864, it was announced that a Bill was to be submitted to Parliament for a bridge of sixty-three spans. Opposition came immediately from the Town Council and the Harbour Board. To pacify the latter the line of the bridge was amended and it was modified to eighty smaller spans. Among other demands, the Town Council insisted that the bridge should carry a footway. The opposition of the Harbour Board remained implacable, fearing a loss of business and an obstruction to navigation. By the time the Bill was submitted to Parliamentary scrutiny in 1866 the North British Railway had come aboard with enthusiasm, and even the Caledonian showed a serious interest, but possibly merely to keep their options open. There followed a period of intense activity, each party jockeying to safeguard, and, if possible, enhance its own interests.

Then came an intervention from the Perth Harbour Trust and its alleged 'large fleet of ships'. The fact of the matter was that for many years they had failed to attend to the dredging of the Tay above Newburgh, and no ship of any size could reach Perth, goods having to be landed at Newburgh and conveyed by shallow draft boats, road, or latterly rail. Perth successfully lobbied the Board of Trade, which bowed to this dog-in-the-manger pressure and declared a bridge to be undesirable. The bridge protagonists at once sent a strong delegation to London, which pointed out the fallacies, if not downright lies, in the Perth argument. The Board of Trade now did a U-turn and approved the bridge plans, subject to certain conditions affecting spans and heights. Luckily the Admiralty had no navigational interests in the Tay Estuary and did not interfere as they did later on the Forth at Queensferry.

One totally unjustifiable demand by Perth was for a clearance of 100ft under the girders at high water over the navigational channels. Few vessels with masts higher than this ventured up even to Newburgh, and Perth was quite inaccessible for them. In addition, an experienced crew could lower or raise a topmast in a matter of minutes when the situation demanded. This was recognised when the second bridge came to be built, and a clearance of 80ft was accepted as adequate. The unfortunate effect of the extra height was to reduce the stability of the bridge in a high wind, thus eventually contributing to its destruction.

The various objectors continued to oppose the bridge, but the North British Railway, and its Chairman, Richard Hodgson, were determined to press ahead, scenting great benefits for the Company. At this juncture the financial crash of 1866 caused the NBR finances to fall into a parlous state approaching insolvency. As conditions improved, Bouch and others continued negotiations, and by 1868 the various objections were overcome by mutual agreement – it might be fair to say that common sense finally prevailed – though there were still doubts as to the actual line of the bridge. Bouch's plans had received the approval of the eminent engineers, J.M. Heppel and T.E. Harrison, though his estimate of £350,000 was considered over optimistic by many of the legion of doubters, which included a number of North British shareholders.

Matters now came to a head, and on 25 November 1868 a public meeting was convened in Dundee Town Hall by Provost Yeaman, when Patrick Mathew, the Seer of Gourdie Hill and a well-known local eccentric, tried without success to frighten those present with awful warnings of disasters and earthquakes. By this stage the general feeling had become favourable to the project. At a meeting of North British shareholders held in Edinburgh on 10 February 1869, a motion to support the Directors in pressing ahead with the bridge was passed by a large majority. Similarly, at a meeting of the Dundee Chamber of Commerce in March 1870 only one dissenting voice was raised. Two days latter the Bill was before a Select Committee of the House of Commons, and their approval was given on 1 April. On 28 June 1870 the Bill went before a Committee of the House of Lords where it was unopposed, and the Royal Assent was given on 15 July. It had been a long and weary road for Bouch and the promoters, and still no end was in sight.

The Building of the Bridge

In the nine years between 1864 and 1873 Bouch had been forced to change the design of his bridge several times to try and reconcile the various vested interests, but it had been uphill work, for when one objector was satisfied another immediately complained of being disadvantaged. Even the site for the bridge was contentious and had to be changed several times. The basic concept survived more or less in its original form, and was finally made public in an article in *The Engineer* published on 4 April 1873. Not only was the design shown in much detail, but a folding panoramic view of the full length of the bridge was included. Bouch must have been highly satisfied with what he read, and he continued to receive support from this particular source up until the time of its fall, when *The Engineer* proved to be a fair-weather friend.

There was nothing unusual in the design except for its length, and Bouch himself modestly described it as 'a very ordinary undertaking'. Even if the rock bed had extended the width of the Firth it was, at least for the contractors, no ordinary undertaking, for the Firth of Tay was seldom without wind, and severe gales were commonplace. As the channel narrowed westwards towards the site of the bridge, tides were fierce, with only short periods of slack water when the caissons for the piers could be placed in position. Small wonder that they were not all perfectly positioned. And of course there was the cold in winter and short hours of daylight. As work fell behind, electric lighting in the form of arc lamps supplied by a steam-driven generator was introduced.

The girders were of wrought iron with riveted joints, and were assembled on site at Dundee from parts fabricated at Middlesbrough. When completed they were floated out on pontoons and lifted into their final place on the piers. The design of the girders was entrusted to a young civil engineer with an honours degree in mathematics from Cambridge, Allan Duncan Stewart, who acted as structural consultant. Bouch had parted from R.H. Bow some time after completion of the Stainmore viaducts, and in any case Stewart was far better qualified. However, Bouch had been persuaded by Bow to use the double triangular or X-type bracing, and he adhered to this throughout his later career. It was probably the most favoured form during the latter part of the nineteenth century until American truss designs started to creep in after 1880. Bouch also continued with a span/depth ratio of eight, which resulted in a very stiff structure.

The piers were planned to be sunk with 10ft diameter iron caissons taken down to the rock by manual excavation under air pressure. In soft ground piling might be needed, and a young Dutchman, Gerrit Camphuis, with extensive experience of pile driving, was recruited to oversee this. Once in their final position the caissons were lined with 14in of brickwork, and infilled with concrete to above high water level when they were continued to the required height in masonry. It was to supervise this that the indefatigable Henry Noble was brought up from London with a glowing reference from Joseph Bazalgette. Cast-iron bedplates fitted with expansion rollers topped the brickwork. All in all, a very simple and satisfactory design. Boulders, some weighing many tons, were encountered by the cutting edges of the caissons, causing them to tilt from the vertical, and were a frequent problem, requiring blasting where they lay. Excavation of the silt within the caissons was greatly speeded up when Frank Beattie, one of the contractor's engineers, devised a steam-driven sand pump.

In his search for economies, Bouch chose a trade-off between span length and the cost of piers. Thus, as the depth of water increased, making piers more expensive, this greater cost could be offset by longer spans. The resulting motley selection of spans adopted by Bouch was the subject of criticism, for this did not improve the appearance of the finished structure, but with Bouch costs would always came first. The maximum span length had originally been 200ft over the navigation channels, but faced with the extra cost of iron piers Bouch resorted to eleven spans of 245ft each, and two of 227ft.

Above left: A portrait of Edgar Gilkes taken in 1853. With his brother Gilbert they founded an engineering firm in Middlesbrough, but Gilbert moved to Kendal where he set up as a maker of water turbines. Edgar entered into partnership with Isaac Wilson.

Above right: Isaac Wilson JP in 1892. For many years he partnered Edgar Gilkes, trading as Gilkes, Wilson & Co. During this time they erected the magnificent iron viaducts at Belah and Deepdale from components prefabricated at the Middlesbrough factory.

A load test on the completed Tay Bridge prior to an inspection by Major-General Hutchinson on behalf of the Board of Trade. This shows very clearly the brick columns used up to Pier 15 at which point the hard bottom was lost after a misleading survey.

The construction site at Wormit, with the foundry on the high bank behind. A completed girder and a number of cast-iron columns can be seen on the erection staging on the right.

As early as 5 October 1869 Bouch had sought the advice of the Board of Trade on wind loadings, and Colonel Yolland informed him that they did not take account of wind pressures with open lattice spans not exceeding 200ft. Perhaps when he increased the spans by 25% Bouch should have thought again, although, apparently unknown to him, Allan Stewart had allowed for 20psf wind loading in his calculations. There was so little understanding of wind forces among engineers of the day that Stewart had relied on experiments carried out by Smeaton a century before. Several years later, with the design of the Forth Bridge in mind, Bouch consulted the Astronomer Royal on the subject of wind pressures, and was advised that an average of 10psf maximum might be expected, with up to 40psf over a narrow front, especially in Scotland.

Even before receipt of the Royal Assent, contract documents and specifications had been sent out to a number of contractors, though many were not prepared to tender for such a major undertaking. The great contractor, Thomas Brassey, was abroad on business, but his agent in Edinburgh, John Milroy, quoted £289,000. Had his tender succeeded the story of the bridge might have ended very differently. The lowest bidders, Butler & Pitts, were awarded the contract, but Pitts, the 'moneyed partner' died shortly afterwards and the firm withdrew. On 8 May 1871 a contract was signed with Charles De Bergue & Co., of London, Manchester and Cardiff, for a contract price of £217,099 18s 6d, clearly a firm which prided itself on its precise estimating, with completion in three years. The firm had considerable experience in building large bridges in this country and abroad, but De Bergue's health was already in decline and work was left to his staff engineers.

It is fair to say that they were experienced and competent men, though lacking in knowledge of foundry work. Why De Bergue chose to build his own foundry at Wormit is not clear, for there were adequate foundries in Dundee quite capable of undertaking the work at a competitive price. It turned out to be a false economy and good moulders and foremen were scarce. Nor was there any fresh water at the chosen site. In addition, many of the faults subsequently found in the hollow cast-iron columns may be attributed to the choice of horizontal casting when vertical casting would have given a better-quality product.

The first of the High Girders under erection at the Dundee end. This picture is of particular interest as the two standing figures are said to be Bouch on the right and Groethe on the left. Note the temporary gas pipe for the navigation lights.

One of the 31ft diameter wrought-iron caissons on its special pontoon ready for floating out. The vertical angle irons with holes were used with hydraulic arms (with the bowler-hatted engineer leaning on one) to lower the caisson to the river bed.

A completed girder waiting to be floated out on two pontoons. The erection gantry has been withdrawn to the left ready for the next girder.

The erection staging at Wormit with the lifting gantry. Two sections of the deck could be removed to allow pontoons to be floated in under the finished girder. Sections of girder sent up from Middlesbrough can be seen lying on the deck in preparation.

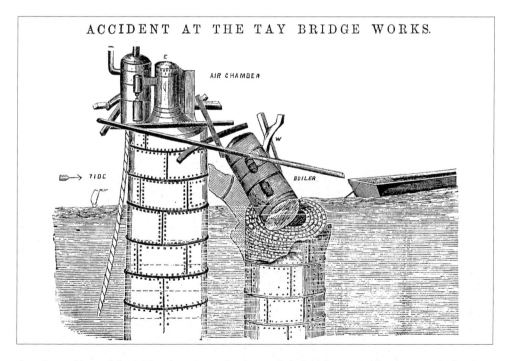

A major accident while sinking the caissons for the north end of the Tay Bridge. Six men died and the unreliability of cast iron was amply demonstrated. After this all caissons were made of wrought iron, a far tougher material under stress.

Heading De Bergue's team were Albert Groethe, a German by birth, and Frank Beattie, his chief draughtsman and assistant. In the drawing office set up at Dundee were the Delpratt brothers, William and Theodore, sent over from Holland to learn their profession. Although Gerrit Camphuis had been sent up to the Tay to advise on piledriving, most of his time was taken up with other duties. A clash of personalities between Groethe and Beattie did not contribute to a smooth-running operation.

Bouch's supervisory staff were thin on the ground. William Paterson, the resident engineer, was a conscientious man, but his experience was limited when it came to supervising the building of the world's longest iron bridge. No doubt his services were inexpensive which would have recommended him to Bouch. For assistance he was given a string of Bouch's articled pupils, including young William Bouch, but most supervision was provided by inspectors at foreman level. The most useful of these was Henry Noble, recruited as an inspector of brickwork but willing – perhaps too willing – to turn his hand to anything demanded of him. In the event he did not have a lot of brickwork to inspect. After completion, maintenance of the whole structure was delegated to him with unfortunate consequences. On one occasion, when there was a shortage of dynamite in Dundee, he was said to have collected it from whatever sources he could, paid for it with his own money, and carried it back through Dundee hidden in his shirt. This was a serious offence if caught, but typical of Noble's conscientious attitude to his duties.

Though it was rumoured that there was rock not far below the sand of the river bed, Bouch employed an experienced mineral borer to check this. At Charlestown in 1864 borings had gone down over 200ft without hitting a firm bottom. On the Tay the borers apparently hit hard ground at no great depth except for a short distance at the Dundee end. This was what Bouch wanted to hear, and he planned his piers accordingly. Never was a man more unintentionally deceived. The Tay Valley, like that of the Forth, was of glacial origins and consisted of a deep channel scoured in the rock, and later filled with glacial detritus in the form of silt but also containing large boulders brought down by floods. What appeared to the borers to be rock was a layer of coarse gravel which had formed into a hard conglomerate several feet in thickness, a relic of a massive flood in prehistoric times when a glacial moraine had burst.

Laying of the foundation stone was a very low-key affair, and took place at Wormit on Saturday 22 July 1871. Apart from Bouch himself there was Sheriff Munro of Kinross, the Revd Mr Thomson of Forgan, and William Paterson, the newly appointed resident engineer, accompanied by his young son who performed the customary taps on the stone. And of course Albert Groethe representing the contractor. Mr Thomson said an appropriate prayer, drams were taken, Sheriff Munro said a few suitable words, and it was all over. A number of workmen, marshalled by Groethe at a respectful distance, cheered on cue, and were later regaled with beer. Whether or not invited to undertake the responsibility, the Revd Thomson deemed himself to be the chaplain of the Tay Bridge Undertaking thereafter.

For the moment all seemed to be set fair, but Charles De Bergue was an increasingly sick man mentally, and was too ill to sign the contract in person. Before long his mental state became worse, but Groethe had sufficient standing in the business to carry on with the bridge. De Bergue died in April 1873, leaving the control of the business in the hands of his wife, Sophia Ring, and his daughter, Anne Mary. The two women strove valiantly to keep the business going, but found to their dismay that the financial position was untenable. De Bergue had put in a low and unrealistic tender to secure the work, and it was impossible for them to carry on, even though Bouch offered them every assistance that he could. He was forced to recommend that the contract should be terminated. Groethe suggested that the bridge should be built by direct labour, with himself as Manager. This proposal was not well received by the NBR Directors, who insisted that Bouch should find a new and reliable firm of experienced contractors.

In desperation, Bouch turned to Edgar Gilkes of Hopkins, Gilkes & Co. of Middlesbrough. They had done an excellent job on the Stainmore line viaducts, which were widely praised, and were an early example of prefabrication on a large scale. Edgar Gilkes and his brother Gilbert had by the middle of the nineteenth century built up a substantial business on Teesside with their own blast furnace, foundry, puddling furnaces and a wrought-iron rolling business. Gilbert went off to Kendal to found the firm of Gilbert Gilkes & Gordon, specialising in small and medium-size water turbines. Edgar entered into a partnership with an investor of the name of Wilson and, trading as Gilkes, Wilson & Co., the business continued to grow and flourish. The personal relationship between Bouch and Gilkes was perhaps too close to be desirable. Gilkes was not only an ironmaster but had more practical experience of iron bridge design than had Bouch. In fact, Gilkes and Groethe contributed much to the rise and fall of the Tay Bridge, and Bouch can perhaps be faulted for delegating too freely.

It was a condition of the new contract that Hopkins, Gilkes & Co. (Hopkins being a new partner in place of Wilson) should take over De Bergue's staff and equipment to maintain continuity, otherwise the casting would probably have been done in their well-equipped foundry at Middlesbrough. All the wrought ironwork was prefabricated there and sent up to Dundee for final assembly.

The immediate crisis was over, but worse was to come. The first fourteen piers on the southern side were constructed in brick, in pairs, each of 10ft diameter, founded on what was believed to be rock. At the fifteenth pier disaster struck. They broke through the hard layer, and found below an unknown depth of gravel, silt and boulder clay, but no firm bottom could be found. With such a foundation the heavy brick piers had to be scrapped, and a broader base used to spread the pressure. A single wrought-iron caisson, 31ft in diameter, was used for each pier, and sunk to a depth where no further movement took place. The caisson was then lined with three courses of brickwork taken up to a couple of feet above high water level, and finally infilled with concrete.

On top of the brickwork were laid four 15in courses of dressed and faced Carmyllie sandstone, and the joints made with a 1:1 cement and sand mixture only about ⅛in in thickness. The unintended effect was that the mortar was so much stronger than the stone that, during the fall, the mortar pulled away from the face of the stone, taking the surface of the stone with it, and was left in large sheets.

The design of the replacement iron piers seems to have been thrashed out at site meetings between Bouch, Gilkes and Groethe, with the details of the diagonal ties being calculated by Allan Stewart, who had, as it was later shown, done a very fine job in the design of the lattice girders. Bouch was concerned about the stability of the piers, and originally placed four columns directly under the girders, with two outriggers each side, but a close examination showed that a single stronger outrigger each side would give a broader base. The final design included four 15in columns supported by a single 18in column each side. In effect this formed two tripods firmly braced together. The diagonal ties which braced the whole structure were flat wrought-iron bars bolted to lugs cast into the columns. Not a good design considering the unreliability of cast iron in tension, but generally acceptable to most engineers at the time in question.

Without giving away too much about the error in the borings, Bouch persuaded the Directors that the replacement of brick by iron piers would cost less. To economise he substituted eleven 245ft and two 227ft girders for the navigation spans instead of using 200ft girders as originally proposed He agreed to a suggestion by Groethe that 1⅛in bolts should be used in the lugs instead of the 1½in bolts originally specified. This, it was argued, would mean that 1⅛in iron only needed to be ordered at a saving. Bouch grasped eagerly at the supposed saving without counting the cost in loss of strength. It was, as he would remark, 'a matter of money'. Just who, as it was later discovered, had reduced the thickness of the diagonal tie bars from ¾in to ½in has never been brought to light, but a finger of suspicion must point at Gilkes and Groethe. Their firm was tottering on the edge of bankruptcy, but this penny-pinching economy may well have become a contributory factor in the fall of the bridge.

There were accidents, though taking into account the size of the undertaking and the difficult conditions, especially in winter, these were surprisingly few. In all twenty men lost their lives. The worst loss of life happened on the night shift of 26 August 1873, when the cast-iron airlock at Pier 54 at the north end of the bridge failed under air pressure, and five of the men working on the bed of the river were drowned by the inrush of water, while a sixth was killed as the steam boiler fell into the river. The engine boy was blown into the water, but swam to a boat and returned to rescue the foreman, the engine driver, and one man who had escaped from below. The boy's name was W. White, and he deserves to be remembered for his heroism. Thereafter wrought iron was used for airlocks though the cause of the premature failure was never discovered. Once again cast iron had proved treacherous.

With the erection of the High Girders almost completed the two southernmost of the girders fell into the river. They had been raised safely into position and left on blocks when, during the night, a high wind blew up, toppling both off their temporary supports. One was too badly damaged to be repaired and had to be replaced, but the second was rebuilt. There were only a few men on the bridge at the time and only one was lost though the foreman suffered a broken leg. In 1877, when work was falling behind, two 500-candlepower arc lights, supplied from a dynamo driven by a 4hp steam engine, were installed to allow work to proceed at night. This is believed to be the earliest occasion on which electric lighting was used to speed up a civil engineering work under construction.

Space does not allow a full description of the building of the bridge, but that ground has been covered more than adequately by authors listed in the bibliography. Bouch had other commitments, including completion of his monstrous proposed bridge over the Forth at Queensferry. He was happy to delegate to William Paterson and others, and placed his faith rather too much in Edgar Gilkes. His firm was encountering severe financial difficulties, and was forced into a complete restructuring in 1880 in order to survive. Survive it did, with Bouch personally paying off a bank loan of £13,000. This resulted from a shareholding left to him when his brother, William Bouch, died. Later the firm grew and prospered until swallowed it was up by British Steel in 1969. It gave more than a century's service to Teesside.

Generally Bouch contented himself with weekly visits, and in the later stages was forced, on his doctor's orders, to take a three-month holiday abroad. He later explained to the Inquiry that the work was going on well and he was not needed on site.

The first train to cross the bridge, a contractor's train, was on 26 September 1877. Bouch had forbidden trains to cross until all the bracing of the piers had been tightened up. Passenger trains had to await the Board of Trade inspection. In February 1878, the bridge was virtually complete except for the final painting. Four coats of best oil paint had been decreed by the specification. There is a suspicion that a black bituminous paint was used instead of linseed oil, thus making it impossible to give a white finishing coat as advised by General Hutchinson to reduce heat absorption and expansion.

Major-General Charles Scrope Hutchinson RE, was sent by Colonel Yolland, Chief Inspecting Officer since 1877, to inspect the bridge on behalf of the Board of Trade. He was blessed with fine weather, and being a very conscientious officer with twelve years experience as an Inspector, he made a very thorough examination of the bridge spread over three days. The High Girders were tested with six heavy goods locomotives, buffered up to create a 50% static overload. These, with their full tenders, weighed some 75 tons each, a total of about 450 tons, compared with the minimum working load advised by Colonel Yolland of 306 tons or 1¼ tons per foot run. A series of live load tests followed with four locomotives coupled together and running over the girders at speeds up to 40mph. These tests were unusually severe but Allan Stewart's girders passed both tests with flying colours, and the General was impressed by the small deflections shown. He also stood on the base of one of the piers with his arms around a column while the locomotives thundered overhead, and was highly satisfied at the lack of vibration. However, he was a cautious man by nature, and recommended that there should be a speed limit of 25mph at all times. He expressed disappointment that he had been unable to observe the behaviour of the bridge in a high wind, and this saved him from criticism when he, and the Board of Trade in the person of Henry Law CE, were giving evidence at the 1880 Inquiry. Hutchison had intended to return, but was taken ill and nobody in Court was tactless enough to ask Colonel Yolland why he had failed to send another Inspector to make the examination.

The official opening of the bridge took place on 31 May 1878, with much celebration in Dundee. Anyone of any consequence in connection with the bridge was there, but strangely, or perhaps characteristically, Bouch himself was not present, even though he was due to be presented with the Freedom of Dundee. It was explained that he had gone south to recuperate after his labours. Earlier in the week he had been visiting English steelmakers, to discuss the material for the chains of the Forth Bridge. In his diary for 31 May Bouch recorded 'Opening of Tay Bridge. Holiday'. It was well deserved.

Apart from through expresses from Burntisland, it was hoped that the bridge would attract commuter traffic from Newport which previously had to depend on ferries. A fortnight before the opening of the bridge the line from Tayport and Newport was opened, and Dugald Drummond, the Locomotive Superintendent, had ordered several small 0-4-2 tank engines with 4ft 6in driving wheels for the bridge traffic. These little engines had a fair turn of speed, well in excess of Hutchinson's 25mph limit, and the drivers were tempted, unofficially of course, to race the ferries which could be seen leaving Newport. There were no problems with the trains going south. The climb from Dundee up to the High Girders limited the speeds which could be attained. From the south side of the Tay the higher banks meant that the rise up to the High Girders was much less, and speeds of over 40mph could be achieved, requiring sharp braking when the curve at the Dundee end of the bridge was reached. This had been anticipated and the bridge strengthened at this point with heavier bracing and outriggers. On the straight run over the High Girders no problems were anticipated after General Hutchinson's satisfactory tests.

10

THE BRIDGE IN SERVICE

As the bridge approached completion towards the end of 1877, Bouch prepared himself for an inspection of the structure by an Inspector from the Board of Trade. There were still many minor matters requiring attention, and by September there were thirty painters employed by a contractor from Sunderland, but they had many months of work ahead of them though that would not delay the inspection. It was critical that all the ironwork should be finished, and the tightening of the rather primitive gib and cotter tensioning device in each bracing bar completed before any trains ran across the bridge. These ensured the rigidity of the piers and the stability of the bridge.

Bouch was well aware of the vital importance of this work. Waddell was engaged in excavating the tunnel beside the harbour wall at Dundee, and put pressure on Groethe for permission to run trains of excavated material across the bridge for disposal on the south bank, with the use of his own locomotive. Groethe must have wisely consulted Bouch, for on 14 August 1877 Bouch wrote him an uncompromising letter:

> I dare not risk an engine on the bridge until the ties are properly tightened and bear their share of the strain. If any idea were entertained of running an engine on before this is done I would immediately resign the engineership to escape responsibility and, moreover, I would consider it my duty to report the matter to the Procurator Fiscal.

This must have been done over the next six weeks, for by 26 September a Directors' special was the first train to cross the bridge amid scenes of much jubilation. There was now no reason why goods trains could not use the bridge, at the Company's risk, since the jurisdiction of the Board of Trade extended only to use by passenger services.

The official opening ceremony took place on 31 May 1878 at Dundee. It had been hoped that Queen Victoria might grace the event with her presence but she wished to maintain her seclusion at Balmoral and declined the opportunity. The official party from Dundee took a ferry across the Tay and a train to Leuchars, where they met the contingent from Edinburgh. There the trains, all of first class coaches, were combined and, with some 600 guests aboard, made their way back over the bridge to Dundee, to be welcomed on arrival by Provost Robertson. Six hundred of the more favoured guests sat down to a banquet at the Albert Hall, but Bouch was not among them.

The Town Council had decided to confer the Freedom of the Burgh on Thomas Bouch at a ceremony before the banquet started, but he was nowhere to be found. Hating these ceremonial occasions he had either slipped quietly away, or had not even been in Dundee that day. It was said on his behalf that, with the bridge completed, he had gone to recruit his health in the South of England where he would be working on his designs for the Forth Bridge. His diary records that earlier in the week Bouch had been visiting English steelmakers to discuss the high-tensile steel chains for his Forth Bridge.

Public train services over the bridge commenced on 1 June, and even with the inconvenience of the Granton to Burntisland ferry crossing, the NBR was able to cut an hour off the best Caledonian time from Edinburgh to Dundee via Stirling and Perth.

Growing Problems with the Bridge

James Bell, civil engineer of the NBR, had been responsible for the laying of the permanent way over the bridge and had done an excellent job. He had naturally expected that he would be given the duty of maintaining the bridge after it had been handed over to the Company on completion. To his dismay (or maybe relief) he was informed that Bouch had offered to take on this work for a fee of 100 guineas (£105) a year. The Company was to supply the supervision and the labourers and pay them. The job of foreman was given to Henry Noble whose limited knowledge of ironwork had rubbed off on him while working on other duties on the bridge. There was no doubt that Noble would take his responsibilities seriously, for that was in his very nature, as Bouch knew.

Noble's first concern was with evidence of tidal scouring around certain of the piers, and particularly where one of the fallen girders had been left lying on a sandbank where it was partly exposed at low water. He determined to remove this but needed dynamite and none could be had in Dundee. This did not deter him and, in his own words:

> I had to go personally with my man to various quarries and beg it, and as there is a heavy penalty if it's known you are carrying it through a town, great secrecy had to be adopted. In fact very few persons know what we have been about, and I paid for everything in connection with the job in ready cash. It was the best and only method I could adopt to get over the affair quietly and economically.

Having done this, and removed as much as possible for scrap, he allowed small sections to fall to the bed of the river (where they probably still lie). Noble then organised the depositing of some 5,000 tons of stone rubble around the affected piers. But there were signs of possible trouble to come. Men working on the bridge, the painters and those laying a 6in water main to Wormit and Newport, talked among themselves of how the bridge vibrated when a train passed, but they were not alarmed and thought that it was not their place to report it. Noble paid little attention to the ironwork until one day in October 1879 when he was working on a pier while a train passed overhead. He had already encountered missing bolts and rivets and had them replaced, but now he heard a chattering noise in some of the tiebars and on examination found that they had worked loose, as he thought, due to slackening of the gib and cotter tensioning devices. Further application of a 4lb hammer proved useless and on his own initiative, and without reference to Bouch, he purchased 22lb of iron bar from a local ironmonger, and over a period cut about 150 wedges to fill the gaps. This temporarily cured the slackness, but it did not occur to Noble to further investigate the cause. When he sent the invoice for the iron to his employers it was paid without query. Neither Noble nor the clerk in Edinburgh realised the hidden implication that the loss of tension arose from bending of the tie bolts. With the best of intentions Noble had unwittingly contributed to the fate of the bridge.

The High Girders completed, showing the gas navigation lights. The tubular handrails doubled up as gas pipes. Although when seen from a distance the bridge was criticised for its apparent lightness, the girders had ample reserves of strength.

A Directors' special train crosses the Tay Bridge on 26 September 1877. There was a lot of tidying up to be done at Wormit before the bridge opened on 29 May the following year, and the line connecting Wormit to Tayport was not yet started.

Important Visitors

As the longest bridge yet built the Tay Bridge attracted attention worldwide, and visitors came from far and wide to sail under it and later to take a train over it. The name of Thomas Bouch was in the Press and, at least in Dundee, on everybody's lips. Fame indeed for the son of a country publican, and a cause of envy and jealousy among certain of his professional brethren.

While the bridge was still under construction there had been many visiting parties of engineers and others with a professional interest, and Groethe was never happier than when showing them around 'his' bridge. There were notabilities too such as the aged Emperor of Brazil, and the convivial Captain Wentzel of the Royal Horse Guards of the King of Holland. There was General Delpratt from Holland, whose two nephews were learning their profession under Groethe's supervision. Some time before, when one of the brothers had proudly shown drawings of the bridge to his uncle, the old General sadly shook his head and said, 'My boy, that bridge will never stand.' Prince Leopold, Queen Victoria's youngest son, visited the bridge in September 1877 when it was nearing completion. On this occasion Bouch had no option but to be present to entertain the royal guest, who asked many questions and expressed his admiration not only for 'the elegance of the bridge, but its solid substantiality'.

In the same month, on 1 September, ex-President of the United States, who had received the credit for winning the Civil War, General Ulysses Simpson Grant — as good a Scots name as could be wished for — came up to Tayport, accompanied by his wife and youngest son, on a special train from Burntisland, and there they were greeted by a reception party of local worthies. They then boarded the tug *Excelsior* under the nominal command of Albert Groethe, and set out for a short tour of the bridge. On the way the nearby training ship *Mars* was visited, where the boys were drawn up on deck or manning the yards. The commander, Captain Scott, invited the General to address the boys, but he was a man of few words, and it was left to Sir John Falshaw of the NBR. After three hearty cheers from the boys the visitors returned to *Excelsior* and the tug headed towards the bridge. Groethe was in his element explaining everything to the General, whose thoughts, it was said, appeared to be more on his delayed lunch.

As might be expected, Bouch, if in town, lunched elsewhere. After a number of toasts had been drunk, Bouch's health was proposed, but when there was a call for Bouch to reply Groethe answered on his behalf. After the formalities, the General was invited to take a walk on the bridge, with the ladies going ahead on a decorated wagon. He had little choice but to agree, though he displayed little enthusiasm, much as he had done all day. To round off the visit Edgar Gilkes made a short speech, and presented the General with a leather album of photographs of the bridge, taken by Mr Valentine, the well-known photographer of Dundee. Asked to comment on his visit, the General was stuck for inspiration and he could only remark, 'It's a very long bridge'. Returning to land, a carriage took the General down to the docks where the party boarded *Excelsior* for the return trip to Tayport, and Edinburgh.

The only event now needed to demonstrate royal approval of the bridge was a visit from Her Majesty Queen Victoria, and in June 1879 it was known that she was due to return from Balmoral to Windsor at the end of the month. She would normally have taken the Caledonian route through Forfar and Perth to Stirling. A hint must have reached Balmoral, for the Queen's personal coach arrived at Dundee from Ballater, and a return gauging trip was made over the bridge without incident. A delegation of three Baillies (Magistrates), all in their Sabbath best and representing the Town Council, set out for Balmoral with a humble petition inviting Her Majesty to break her journey at Dundee to receive a Loyal Address, before crossing the bridge. This time Bouch had received his orders from Provost Yeoman, one of the NBR Directors and the letter read:

> I am sure that it is unnecessary for me to remind you of your position as engineer of the bridge that Her Majesty will receive every attention for her comfort and safety, and it will be expected that you will accompany the Royal Train from the time it enters until it leaves the North British system.

Everybody who was anybody in Dundee had turned out in their uniforms or finest clothes to greet the Queen. Those who could not find room on the station lined the streets. Bandsmen grew purple in the face trying to outdo their rivals.

The Royal Train, pulled by a Caledonian engine, arrived at Tay Bridge Station at 5.57 p.m., and was timed to stop for seven minutes while the North British engine 'Netherby' was attached.

A panoramic view of the completed Tay Bridge, seen from Magdalen Green, Dundee. The extraordinary lightness of the bowstring girder in the foreground calls for comment though no drawings are available. Bouch built a very similar bridge at Maidstone.

NORTH BRITISH RAILWAY COMPANY.

M
No. 789.

EDINBURGH, *28th May 1878.*

Notice to Enginemen, Guards, Signalmen, and others.

Opening of Tay Bridge for General Traffic.

In anticipation of the Opening for General Traffic, the following Regulations for the working of the Tay Bridge will be brought into force at 12 o'clock Noon on

WEDNESDAY, 29th MAY, 1878.

The Tay Bridge will be worked as one Section, under the combined systems of Block Telegraph and Train Staff and Train Ticket, as follows:—

I. By Block Telegraph.

All Trains and Engines must be signalled in strict accordance with the Revised General Instructions for Working Trains over Single Lines by Tyers' Telegraph Signal—dated 18th August 1873.

SPECIAL NOTE.—This Section is specially excepted from the operation of Clause 11 of the General Instructions above referred to, and therefore a Second Train or Engine *must not* be allowed to follow before the first Train or Engine has been signalled Clear.

II. By Train Staff and Train Ticket.

The Section will be worked by Train Staff and Train Ticket, in accordance with the Rules for working Single Lines of Railway by Train Staff and Train Ticket system, as contained in the Company's Book of Rules and Regulations, at pages 57 to 63 inclusive.

The Colour of Train Staff and Train Tickets will be Dark Blue, and the No. of the Train Staff is No. 4.

The Signalmen at Tay Bridge South and Tay Bridge North Cabins will be the custodiers of the Train Staff and Train Tickets. Before giving the Driver of a Train or Engine the Train Staff or Train Ticket, the Signalman at the one Cabin must be careful to signal on the Train by Block Telegraph to the other Cabin; and until such Signal has been given, and properly acknowledged, by the needle being turned to " Train on Line," the Signalman must not part with either the Train Ticket or Train Staff.

In the event of the failure of the Block Telegraph Instruments, an interval of 15 minutes must be maintained between all trains until the Block Telegraph is again in operation; and great caution must be exercised by all concerned.

Speed of Trains and Engines passing over Tay Bridge.

The Speed of Trains and Engines, when passing over the Tay Bridge, must never exceed the following limits:—

	Speed must not exceed
Passenger Trains and Light Engines ...	25 Miles an Hour.
Goods, Cattle, and Mineral Trains ...	20 ,, ,,
Ballast Trains	15 ,, ,,

Simultaneously with the commencement of the above arrangements, the mode of working the Tay Bridge by Red Cap Pilotman presently in operation will be discontinued.

(1000)

J. WALKER,
General Manager.

Acknowledgment to be signed, cut off, and returned to General Superintendent's Office, Edinburgh, by first Train.

Date _____ _____ 1878.

Official notice of the Opening of the Tay Bridge on 29 May 1878. On this day operation of the single-line bridge by train staff and block telegraph was introduced. Note particularly a restatement of the speed limits to be observed by all trains.

Queen Victoria's only trip across the Tay Bridge was on a Friday afternoon in June 1879 when returning from Balmoral to Windsor. Bouch was on the footplate while traversing NBR lines and was presented to the Queen during the stop at Dundee.

Provost Brownlee read the loyal address and handed the vellum scroll to the Queen who accepted it graciously and passed it to one of her ladies-in-waiting. John Stirling, James Cox and Thomas Bouch were briefly presented to Her Majesty. At 6.04, with a whistle from 'Netherby', the Royal Train slowly left the platform and within two minutes entered the bridge where it slowed, taking twice the normal time to cross so that Her Majesty could enjoy the view, but the Queen's thoughts may have been elsewhere. She had received news only that morning of the death in the Zulu Wars of Leopold, Prince Imperial of France and the son of Napoleon III. But she and her Private Secretary, Sir Henry Ponsonby, did not forget the man whose brainchild the Tay Bridge was, and within a few days Bouch received instructions to present himself at Windsor Castle on Thursday 29 June to receive a knighthood. No doubt he hated it, but Margaret Terrie Bouch was equally overjoyed to become Lady Bouch.

Complaints from Passengers

A number of Dundee men of business had built houses at Wormit and Newport and relied on the ferries to reach Dundee. With the opening of the bridge further development was expected, as previously the shortage of fresh water had delayed this, pending provision of a new pipeline over the bridge to carry water from Dundee. There was no doubt that the train was more comfortable, but a number of passengers complained of excessive speed over the High Girders. Among these was ex-Provost William Robertson, owner of a foundry in Dundee. The heavier trains from Burntisland kept within the speed limit, but the lighter local trains, pulled by small 0-4-4 tank engines which Dugald Drummond had designed originally for the Clyde coast services, soon showed that they were capable of a fair turn of speed. Racing the Newport ferry became common practice and bets were laid. One train, timed by ex-Provost Robertson, reached 43mph, and on arrival at Dundee he lodged a strong complaint of a rough ride with the stationmaster, James Smith. The stationmaster had no authority over the running of trains and was unwilling to tackle Dugald Drummond in his den. He did mention it to the locomotive foreman at Dundee, but without effect, for he too feared Drummond's temper. After three unsatisfied complaints Robertson reverted to the ferry for his northbound journeys.

While the Robertson family refused to use the bridge, the family of John Leng, newspaper proprietor, were less timid and Leng himself declared that only about one train in ten was guilty of speeding. In any case, the motion of the carriage which so distressed Robertson was dismissed by Leng as a prancing motion like being on horseback and nothing to cause alarm. Those painters still working on the bridge were conscious of increasing vertical and sideways movement while trains were passing. Little did they realise it but the sideways motion posed the greater danger, for it indicated slackening of the ties with every high wind despite Noble's efforts. After each gale the bridge became progressively weaker and the gale of 28 December 1879 proved to be the last straw. It could have happened sooner or even much later, but it was only a matter of time before the bridge would fall.

The prancing motion was much less serious, and if the 25mph speed limit had been observed it would have vanished. It played no part in the final destruction of the bridge. The reason for this motion was not understood at the time, but to explain it as briefly as possible – every girder has a natural frequency of vibration just as does a violin string. Due to the stiffness of the High Girders their natural frequency was in the region of 3.5Hz which is unusually high. Surprisingly, it was Drummond's small tank locomotives which caused the problem but only when running at over about 40mph. Trains leaving Dundee for the south faced a steep climb up to the High Girders, which limited their speed and nothing untoward was noticed. Going north there was a much easier gradient, and the trains could build up speeds of 40mph or more before entering the High Girders.

The tank engines had driving wheels 5ft 9in in diameter though not intended as 'flyers'. A wheel of that diameter has a circumference at the tyre of 18ft and at 43mph revolves at 3.5 times a second. Once at each revolution out of balance forces would deliver a blow to the rail (later known as hammer blow but not until many years after when it was adopted from the work of Indian railway engineers). If each impulse was at the same frequency as the natural period of vibration of the girder it would start to vibrate vertically. Over a 245ft girder there would be 13.6 impulses which would be cumulative and explain the 'prancing motion' observed by John Leng. But though these motions were undesirable for the comfort of passengers, they acted vertically on the piers, which had generous reserves of strength. This phenomenon was probably unfamiliar to Bouch or other engineers of his generation. Today it is known as resonance. The painters, working high up on the girders, knew the effect only too well, and had to tie on their paint cans while they themselves clung on for dear life when certain trains passed.

Despite their earlier reservations, when the bridge was in use the people of Dundee realised what a great boon it was. With greatly increased traffic the NBR shareholders could appreciate what a wise investment it had been, and two new ferries with passenger saloons were introduced on the Forth crossing to improve the service. At 427 gross tons the larger of the two, *John Stirling*, was by far the largest ferry plying the Forth. So large in fact, that it proved necessary to blast rocks in the harbour entrance at Burntisland to allow the vessel to enter the harbour. The first wagon ferry of 1850, *Leviathan*, had been joined by three other boats, but with the increase in traffic after the opening of the Tay Bridge, and even though running throughout the twenty-four hours, they were hard pressed to maintain the service. With the prospect of a Forth Bridge not far away the NBR was reluctant to invest in a new goods ferry.

An undated report in the *Illustrated London News* revealed that Bouch did eventually receive the Freedom of Dundee from the hands of the Provost, presumably at a meeting of the Town Council. It must have been done before he received his knighthood on 26 June 1878 as he is still plain Mr Bouch. In his reply, he said that he believed that it was the first time an engineer had been given the freedom of a city. He expressed a regret that the Tay Bridge had been made for only a single line, and told his listeners that, from experience gained at Dundee, his new bridge over the Forth would be built for a double line.

11

THE LAST TRAIN

The last train on a Sunday evening to Dundee left Waverley after darkness had fallen on the evening of 28 December 1879, and made the short journey to Granton Harbour, from where passengers had to endure the rigours of a ferry to Burntisland. There the Dundee train would be waiting to leave at 5.20 p.m. On that particular evening the usual little 0-4-4 Drummond tank engine was not available, and the spare engine at Burntisland, a Wheatley 4-4-0 passenger engine No. 224, was substituted.

Sunday travel on the North British Railway had always been a contentious issue from the time of opening, and the mainly English shareholders showed little respect for Scottish sensibilities. Sunday railway travel in England had caused much dissension in earlier years, but in the course of time it came to be accepted by most. In Scotland it was a very different situation, with feelings running high, and Sunday travellers were denounced from pulpits throughout the land. Dire warnings were issued of divine wrath and retribution to come for those so impious as to travel on the Sabbath. Despite this, the last train going north on a Sunday evening was usually well patronised by sinners returning home or to be ready for work the next morning.

Among these might have been a young engineer of the name of Brodie, who was employed by John Waddell, the contractor on the Arbroath & Montrose line. On the previous day he had travelled over the bridge to his home near Cupar, some 8 miles to the west. His father was a strict Sabbatarian and would not allow his son to return on the Sunday evening. In his autobiography Brodie described the storm that night as the most terrific in his experience. Just after midnight he was awakened by water pouring in, and found that the flat lead on the roof, weighing over a ton, had been rolled up by the wind and deposited in a nearby field. Furthermore, the mill chimney was destroyed, and the contents of the stackyard scattered far and wide. More remarkably, another stackyard a quarter of a mile away was untouched. The point behind this story is that it shows clear evidence, never reported to the official Inquiry, that hurricane action did take place on the fateful night. Brodie's name appeared next day on the first list of those who had died, and his colleagues were much relieved when he turned up unharmed later on the Monday.

The train left Burntisland and fought its way through the storm until eventually reaching the small station of St Fort on the southern approach to the Tay Bridge. Here it waited while the staff struggled to collect tickets from those going to Dundee. A few were travelling towards Arbroath and, unless their bodies were washed up, could not all be accounted for later. Some reckoned that they had seen several babes in arms and they too, if they ever existed, were lost. One old lady was so agitated that she attempted to leave her compartment, and was locked in by the guard for her own safety. The used tickets were mixed up with those collected earlier in the day, and had to be separated so far as possible later when assessing the deaths.

The previous train to Dundee had crossed the bridge with some difficulty; sparks flying in the wind forced the wheel flanges against the check rails. Since then the gusts had increased, and the St Fort stationmaster would have held the train until the gusts had eased had his authority allowed. The train went on its way, and reached the Wormit signal box where it slowed to walking pace to take the single line baton. From there, the line curved to the north before running on to the open girders so that the full fury of the wind caught the train sideways on. The carriages rocked alarmingly on their springs, especially the small second class coach next to the guard's van and weighing less than six tons. This was the most dangerous part of the crossing, where the line ran unprotected on top of the girders. Once the train entered the High Girders it had a slight degree of protection. Certainly the wheels were grinding and causing sparks, but to those on the footplate it only needed a touch on the regulator to compensate. Even the footplate crew must have felt the locomotive rocking as the wind attacked the girders and caused them to sway with every gust.

There were few eyewitnesses of what took place next, for it was too dark, and those who claimed to have a story to tell were unreliable, anxious for their brief moment of fame. It is likely that just as the locomotive was about to enter the fifth girder an exceptionally fierce gust – a hurricane even – derailed the last two coaches, which were then dragged halfway along the fourth girder, destroying the track as they went. Finally the coupling broke, the two coaches (the second class and the guard's van) were blown over against the side of the bridge, then left the rails altogether and telescoped against the end of the fourth girder, causing a substantial shock to the structure. By this time the front of the train had entered the fifth girder which was already starting to topple sideways by the time that the locomotive had reached the centre of the girder. The locomotive fell with the girder, which turned in its fall causing the locomotive to fall flat on its side, but causing remarkably little damage. The coaches floated up against the falling side of the girder, wrecking the roofs but leaving much of the bodywork intact, until they dropped back on to the side of the fallen girder in an upright position on their wheels. All aboard were flung out and drowned, and the bodies were quickly swept away by the currents.

At Dundee they had received a signal from Wormit shortly after 7.00 p.m. that the train had entered the bridge. At 7.30 p.m. the train had not arrived, and communication with Wormit had been lost. Word quickly spread and crowds were starting to arrive, and with glass flying from the roof the stationmaster gave orders for the station to be closed. Roberts, the locomotive foreman and a former seaman, volunteered to go out to the bridge with Smith, the stationmaster. The latter was forced to turn back, but the heroic Roberts struggled on, clinging to the rails on his hands and knees, until he could go no further. In front of him was a dreadful void with the angry waters of the Tay far below. Water was pouring from a broken water main and was blown away before it could reach the waves beneath. With difficulty Roberts struggled back, with the wind trying to tear his grip away, and spread the message to the waiting crowds. At the Caledonian station their stationmaster rallied round and the telegraph office was opened to allow communications with Perth and Stirling, and from there to Edinburgh and London.

By 10.30 p.m. the storm had eased enough to allow the ferry boat *Dundee*, under the command of Captain Methven, to go out to the bridge, though they dared not approach too closely for fear of the fallen girders. There was nothing to be seen but the twelve stumps of the piers, lashed by the waves. Little could be done before the coming of the dim light of a Dundee winter morning at about 8.00 a.m. The news had reached London and Sir Henry Ponsonby, who had accompanied Queen Victoria over the bridge a few months earlier, sent a telegram:

Wheatley 4-4-0 express locomotive No. 224 after being dragged from the river. Most of the damage is superficial and No. 224 was taken to Cowlairs for rebuilding. Henceforth nicknamed 'The Diver', she remained in service until taken over by the LNER.

The fifth from the south of the High Girders, lying on its side on the beach at Broughty Ferry. The carriages must have floated on entering the water before the roofs were destroyed by the falling girder.

Number 5 of the High Girders lying on the beach at Broughty Ferry, with the remains of the first four coaches still lying inside. owing to its weight, the locomotive had already been removed

Number 2 of the High Girders lying on a sandbank in the Tay. This had suffered a similar fall when a gale blew up while it was being erected. It was reconstructed at Wormit and safely re-erected, but there were doubts about its condition.

A recent view looking towards Dundee showing the pathetic stumps of Bouch's bridge and the massive piers of W.H. Barlow's bridge which replaced it, standing firm today.

> Can you give me any particulars of the appalling calamity reported to have taken place? The Queen is inexpressibly shocked and feels most deeply for those who have lost friends and relatives in this terrible accident.

Already at Dundee voices were being raised condemning Bouch as a charlatan, claiming that the workmen had been drunk, and that the bridge had been against God's will, and in His wrath He had destroyed it. There would be much more of this to come. Meanwhile, though no bodies had as yet been washed up, mailbags were found on the beach at Broughty Ferry. John Stirling and Sir Thomas Bouch had arrived in the early hours. Now it was a priority to find the dead and give them decent burial. Part of the station refreshment room was set aside as a temporary mortuary. Down in London the President of the Board of Trade was echoing the shouts of the crowd in Dundee, and demanding a reason as to why the bridge should have fallen.

Not until darkness was starting to fall on the Monday afternoon was the first body recovered from the river about 3 miles below the bridge and brought to Dundee. Every day, if the weather permitted, boats would continue to scour the river with nets, grappling irons and boathooks. Flotsam covered the foreshore and personal items were salvaged and taken to the temporary mortuary for safekeeping. As the hours passed rumours grew among the waiting crowd and their anger increased against Bouch and his employers, the NBR, as well as the Government in London. It was their Inspecting Officer who had passed the bridge as safe less than two years before.

On the Wednesday evening, three days after the fall, a public meeting took place in the Town Hall. Provost Brownlee first called for subscriptions for a relief fund. He had already received £1,000 from the NBR and donations from individual Directors, to which Bouch had added £250. On the same day the NBR Directors met in Edinburgh, and passed a resolution that the Tay Bridge should be rebuilt – they did not specify by whom – and that all work on the Forth Bridge should cease forthwith. These decisions did not receive universal approbation. One critic wrote:

> Evidently the Directorate of the North British Railway Company is so engrossed with defending their money interest and planning the rebuilding of their fallen structures that they cannot give thought or time how best the dead may be restored to their sorrowing friends. In the name of outraged feelings I call upon the Company to appoint a well-skilled engineer to take charge …

Unfair perhaps, but indicative of the strong public sentiment.

On Thursday, New Year's Day and traditionally a Scottish holiday, the Company offered to pay £5 for every body recovered. Meanwhile, Major Marindin RE of the Board of Trade had come up from London, and had taken a room at the Royal Hotel where Bouch was staying. Marindin was there to hold the fort until an Inquiry could be organised. Friday was too rough for the smaller boats to go out. Saturday dawned bright and fair, and the Inquiry convened at 2.00 p.m. after inspecting the ruins of the bridge. In all, thirty-three bodies were recovered by the end of January, one as far away as the shores of Caithness. The river refused to yield up about twenty-nine victims who were never found.

The final death toll may have been less than reported. Some time later the Dundee Police published a list of only sixty-four names. How this should come about is difficult to say. In those times of grinding poverty some may surely have been tempted to apply to the Relief Fund, which was well in excess of £3,000, for an imaginary relative whose body was entirely lost. Who could disprove it? Even more strangely, missing persons may never have been reported – not such an unusual occurrence even in more recent times. After the Charfield railway accident of 1928 the bodies of two children found in the wreckage were never claimed. No-one will ever know for sure the exact loss of life at the Tay, and although infants were reported at St Fort none were recovered and none appear on the police record.

The Storm in Edinburgh: Bad News for Sir Thomas Bouch

Christmas Day 1879 fell on a Thursday. The Bouchs had probably attended the midnight service at Holy Trinity Episcopal Church on the banks of the Water of Leith, and within easy walking distance of their house at 6 Oxford Terrace. The weather was cold but there was no snow yet for the worst of the winter was still to come. Then, and for the best part of the following century, Christmas Day in Scotland was an ordinary working day, shops and offices were open and newspapers published. Bouch had gone down to his office as usual, for pressure for the final plans for the new Forth Bridge was building up. Young William was about his business in Montrose and looking forward to his break at the New Year, traditionally the main Scottish holiday of the year when no work was done.

The morning of the last Sunday in December 1879 gave little warning of the storm to come, and the Bouch family attended the morning service at Holy Trinity as usual. There were only the four of them now, as Fanny, the elder daughter, had for some time past been married to an Englishman, a Mr Hussey, and had gone south to live in London. Young William Bouch, who had recently completed his pupilage and celebrated his twenty-first birthday, had become a resident engineer on the line from Arbroath to Montrose, a further link in the NBR's grand design of reaching Aberdeen. William planned to stay in Edinburgh over the New Year celebrations and this was to save his life. To the Bouchs, Hogmanay was an event to be celebrated quietly, with no first footing from door to door carrying a piece of coal and being regaled with black bun and whisky. In Scotland, on New Year's Day, there were few who worked and many who were in no fit state to work.

On their way home, facing into the wind which had risen and veered to the west, they noticed that the breeze was increasing in strength and starting to gust. As darkness fell in mid-afternoon the wind started to rattle the front windows in Oxford Terrace which faced open fields. At No. 6 the internal window shutters were closed and barred, and at the front entrance the storm doors firmly secured. Nothing more could be done, and the family and the servants retired early to their beds. The gusts of wind had increased in force during the early evening but gradually eased as midnight approached. It was not an exceptional storm but certainly no night to be out in the streets risking the occasional flying slate, or a chimney can, weakened by frost, tumbling down the slates, falling to the flagstones and shattering into a hundred fragments.

At Dundee, when the steamer *Dundee* under Captain Methven had managed to reach the bridge after an earlier attempt had been abandoned, there came final confirmation that most if not all of the High Girders were down and that no survivors could be found. Since the telegraph circuits across to Fife were broken as the bridge fell, a message was sent over the Caledonian wires through Perth and Stirling, and was received at the NBR St Margaret's depot in Edinburgh because the Head Office in Waterloo Place was bolted and barred. The message was bleak:

> Terrible accident on bridge. One or more of High Girders blown down. Am not sure as to the safety of the last train from Edinburgh. Will advise further as soon as can be obtained [sic].

From the St Margaret's locomotive sheds at Craigentinny to the east of Edinburgh a messenger was sent to John Stirling, Company Chairman, who immediately ordered a special train to be prepared and held ready at Waverley. There was as yet no telephone service in Edinburgh other than two small exchanges in the New Town serving about fifty premises each. Cabs were found with some difficulty late on a stormy Sunday night and were despatched to summon Bouch and the General Manager, John Walker, while Sir John Falshaw, the Deputy Chairman, took charge of events in Edinburgh.

Some time after 11.00 p.m. the Bouch household was roused by a frantic pealing of the front door bell in the basement and a heavy knocking on the outer front door. One of the maids answered the summons. After closing the outer door against the wind which was still gusting strongly, the cabman was let in to the inner hall, where he stood, the rain dripping off him on to the marble tiles. When Bouch came downstairs in his dressing gown, bedroom candlestick in hand, the man blurted out, 'You must come quickly, Sir Thomas. The bridge is down.' Bouch had become somewhat deaf and the man had to repeat the message before it sank in. Like most young men of his age William was a heavy sleeper, but he too was aroused by the commotion below. Lady Bouch and Elizabeth Ann, now a handsome young lady of twenty-three, clung to each other at the head of the stairs. William was told by his father to get dressed, and within minutes he and Sir Thomas were in the cab heading for Waverley Station. There they joined John Stirling and James Walker in the waiting train, and leaving at twenty minutes past midnight they were at Granton Harbour by the half hour.

The wagon ferries ran throughout the twenty-four hours, and the largest, the thirty-year-old *Leviathan*, was waiting with steam up while the foreman at Granton had ballasted it against the rough seas with a number of wagons. After a rough and uncomfortable crossing they found another train waiting at Burntisland, and it quickly set out across Fife to the station at Leuchars. The usual Drummond tank engines built for this service were not available, but one of Wheatley's 4-4-0 express engines made short work of the journey across Fife. There was little talking on the train. Stirling and Walker spoke almost in whispers, Bouch was immersed in his own grim thoughts, and William was realising that on any other weekend of the year he too would have been on that last train from

Edinburgh. At Leuchars there was a brief halt to meet the stationmaster and other officials. They told later how Bouch had been in a pitiful state of mind.

The train headed for Tayport where the little steamer *James Cox* was waiting to cross to Dundee, but the sea was still too rough, and the Newport ferries were all sheltering in Dundee Harbour. After some delay a second attempt met with success. It was still far too early for the first light to reveal the full extent of the tragedy. Once the wind had dropped the sea became quieter, and as dawn broke the steamer *Fairwater* went out with a diver, but after several attempts he reported that the water was too muddy after the storm to see anything. Bouch expressed a wish to see the bridge for himself, and was invited by the captain of the *Forfarshire* to join him about 10.00 a.m. Almost anything that would float had been commandeered to go out to the bridge, and armed with nets, boathooks and grappling irons the boats were searching for bodies but without success until the tide changed. There was little for Bouch to see, except for the gaping void where once twelve massive iron piers had stood, carrying their thirteen heavy girders. Now only the stone bases, largely undamaged, showed above the swirling waters. As the tide fell, one twisted girder, resting on a sandbank, showed where it had fallen eastwards under the force of the wind. There was nothing more that Bouch could do, and faced with some hostility from members of the crowd at Dundee he deemed it best to return to Edinburgh while the recovery of bodies continued.

Once the first fateful telegram had been despatched to Edinburgh, a local Dundee journalist, John Malloch, sent telegrams to the London papers. They arrived too late for the morning editions, but later special editions contained the brief statement that the Tay Bridge had fallen. Malloch's message was short:

> Monday 1.30 a.m. The scene at the Tay Bridge Station tonight is simply appalling. Many thousands of persons are congregated around the building, and strong men and women are wringing their hands in despair ...

Fifty years later, to the day, the same John Malloch, now long retired, wrote an article for the *Dundee Courier and Advertiser* recounting his personal experiences on that momentous night. So too did several local worthies, for to many of the older citizens the 28th of December 1879 was a night never to be forgotten.

From the North British in Edinburgh a message had gone out to the President of the Board of Trade. The Duty Officer who received it had no qualms in sending a messenger to rouse the President, Lord Sandon, third Earl of Harrowby, from his slumbers. This was not only a national tragedy but it had potentially serious political overtones demanding immediate action and attempts at damage limitation from the Government. The Conservatives, led for the last time by Benjamin Disraeli, Lord Beaconsfield, had been in power for nearly five years, but their leader was a sick man with little more than a year to live. The country was in a poor way, in the throes of one of the all too frequent slumps, and a General Election was pending. In February 1878 Major-General C.S. Hutchinson RE had inspected and approved the bridge on behalf of the Board of Trade and embarrassing questions would be asked by the Leader of the Opposition and the Press regarding culpability. There were also doubts as to the quality of the advice given by Colonel Yolland on behalf of the Board of Trade, when approached by Bouch at the design stage some years earlier.

Parliament was dissolved on 24 March 1880 and voting followed a week later. W.E. Gladstone had come out of retirement at the age of seventy-one to lead the Liberals to victory, and he was rewarded with a landslide majority of 115. Whether or not the Tay Bridge affair had any influence is impossible to say. Queen Victoria was mortified, for she had once confided to her dear Lord Beaconsfield that Mr Gladstone addressed her as though she were at a public meeting, and relations between them were always strained.

The formidable Joseph Chamberlain, who, as a reforming Mayor of Birmingham, had given that city sewers twenty years before London had them, was now President of the Board of Trade, and was not a man to be trifled with. Henry Cadogan Rothery, Commissioner of Wrecks, was appointed to head a Public Inquiry, and was under pressure to find a villain or a scapegoat – either would do – to bring the Tay Bridge Inquiry to a satisfactory end. To reassure the public as to the safety of iron bridges would take some while longer.

On Monday the tragic news from Dundee had arrived too late for the morning papers to offer many details but a rumoured loss of 300 innocent lives was already circulating. Before the full impact of the disaster became known on Tuesday morning the Government had to be seen to have taken firm action. Within hours it was announced that a Court of Inquiry would be convened and would start its work in the Assize Court at Dundee the following Saturday, 3 January 1880.

12

THE COURT OF INQUIRY
AND ITS AFTERMATH

In selecting Henry Cadogan Rothery, Commissioner for Wrecks, as Chairman of the Court there was some logic, since it could reasonably be argued that a bridge and a railway train lost in tidal waters came within his jurisdiction. He was a lawyer by training but with a Cambridge degree in mathematics, and was regarded by the Government of the day as a safe pair of hands who knew what was expected of him. His formal instructions were set out as follows, and it should be noted that there is no mention of allocating blame. This was not a Court of Law:

> A formal investigation directed by the Board of Trade, to be held into the causes of, and circumstances attending, the accident to the Tay Bridge, Dundee, on Sunday, 28th December 1879.

Privately, Rothery had been given to understand by his political masters that the Board of Trade and the North British Railway Company were as far as possible to be exonerated in order to reassure public opinion, which was becoming increasingly hostile as one body after another was dragged from the river. Two engineers were appointed as assistant Commissioners. Colonel William Yolland RE, Chief Inspector of Railways, was one. He had joined the Inspectorate in 1854, and died shortly before he was due to retire in 1885 after thirty-one years service – a record. He was described as a colourful and fiery character. His colleague was William Henry Barlow, then the distinguished President of the Institution of Civil Engineers, and at the age of fifty-eight he stood at the peak of his profession. Henry Law CE was appointed as engineering adviser to the Board of Trade, and Dr William Pole CE FRS acted as technical adviser to Bouch.

There was a plethora of lawyers and their hangers-on. Mr Trayner appeared for the Board of Trade, and Mr Balfour for the North British Company, while Bouch was represented by George Parker Bidder, son of Robert Stephenson's old friend of the same name. Mr Webster represented the contractors, and Mr Dunbar held a watching brief on behalf of the Lord Advocate. Under Scottish Law a Fatal Accident Inquiry would need to be held for each of the victims, and this would be the responsibility of the Procurator Fiscal in the Sheriff Court at Dundee after the main Inquiry was completed. The Inquiry proved nothing if not thorough, though much of the time it was chasing red herrings. It sat for twenty-five days, examined 120 witnesses, and asked 19,919 questions. Sir Thomas Bouch was accountable under the law as engineer-in-chief, so it came as no surprise when at the end the full blame was laid on his shoulders, although Rothery exceeded his remit in so doing. Political expediency had been served but whether justice had been done was another question altogether. There is only space here to examine Bouch's own evidence in detail, but more detailed reports are available in several books listed in the bibliography, and of course in the official Report of the Inquiry which runs to some 600 pages.

When the Inquiry convened on 3 January 1880 Bouch was not present, and his assistant, Charles Meik, stood in for him. Mr Rothery expressed a wish to examine the bridge and arrangements were put in hand. Meik was asked for plans of the bridge but explained that he had only a few with him and, not realising that they would be required, had left the rest at his hotel. He was promptly sent packing to fetch them, and since it was a fine day the Court adjourned to visit the wreck of the bridge. Although at first sight there was not a lot of information to be gleaned from the wreckage, the sheer scale of the disaster was immediately apparent. Where once the thirteen great girders had proudly stood 88ft above high water there were now only twelve stumps projecting a few feet above surface, and a bent girder lying on a sandbank and visible at low tide. Of the train there was no sign.

At 2.00 p.m. the Court reconvened, Meik produced his plans, and the questioning of local witnesses began. During the first three days a number of local eyewitnesses were examined together with railway staff and several of the divers. Charles Meik was recalled on the Monday morning and he confirmed that he had now brought all the plans that he could find. The following day the Court adjourned and did not convene again at Dundee until Thursday 26 February. At least the public could see that something was being done, but voices were raised in the streets and some were openly denouncing Bouch as a murderer. In fact, manslaughter was the worst charge that could have been brought.

While the Commissioners were inspecting the remains of the cast-iron piers they noticed the number of broken cast-iron lugs from the vertical columns lying on top of the stonework. These lugs had been cast into the vertical columns of the piers, and to them was attached the wrought-iron diagonal bracing which held the whole structure rigid. This was a perfectly acceptable engineering practice at the time, even though many years earlier William Fairbairn and others had denounced cast iron as a treacherous material when under tension. Most of the columns had buckled or tilted over, breaking up and falling into the sea. The position of the broken lugs suggested that they had failed and dropped vertically before the columns had collapsed sideways. In effect the bracing appeared to have unzipped while the piers failed. Even at this very early stage this was a pointer as to the cause of failure, but there were many alternative scenarios to consider in the light of further evidence.

In the aftermath of the disaster some sympathy for Bouch was expressed in the Press. Sir John Falshaw, Deputy Chairman of the North British, spoke of an act of God. The following Sunday his sentiment was echoed from many a pulpit, even to the extent of declaring that those who desecrated the Sabbath, including the North British Company, had received their just deserts. *The Glasgow Evening Times* wrote:

> Sir Thomas Bouch had necessarily to use his own judgement in regard to points of novelty on which the experience of other engineers would give him but small assistance. His work, taking into account its surprising cheapness, has been universally pronounced a success, and there can be little doubt that it would in ordinary circumstances have become the parent of many similar structures.

The *Glasgow Herald* though had put its oar in first that morning and commented:

> It is easy to be wise after the event, but it must not be forgotten that the melancholy event of last night has been more than once fore-shadowed by the opponents of this great engineering scheme.

No.	Details	Location
1.	Joseph ANDERSON (21) Compositor, Dundee	Cupar
	* 23. 4.80 off Caithness (45)	
2.	Thomas ANNAN (22) Mechanic, Dundee	Newburgh
	* 1. 4.80 Tentsmuir (43)	
4.	Archibald BAIN (26) Farmer, Balgay, Dundee	Cupar
	* 8. 1.80 near bridge (16)	
5.	Jessie BAIN (22) Sister of above " "	Cupar
	* 18. 2.80 near bridge (38)	
6.	William Henry Benyon, photographer, Cheltenham	Edinburgh
	* 7. 2.80 near Newport Pier (34)	
7.	Lizzie BROWN (14) Granddaughter of Mrs Mann, Dundee ,	Leuchars
8.	Mrs CHEAP (50) Domestic Servant, Lochee, Dundee	St Fort
9.	James CRICHTON, Ploughman, Fintry, Dundee	
	* 6. 1.80 near bridge (5)	
10	Annie CRUICKSHANKS (54) Maid to Lady Baxter, Edinburgh	Edinburgh
	* 29.12.79 near Newport (1)	
11.	Robert CULROSS Carpenter, Tayport	Edinburgh
	* 13. 3.80 Monifieth (41)	
12.	David CUNNINGHAM (21) Mason, Lochee, Dundee	St Fort
	* 10. 1.80 near bridge (23)	
14.	Thomas DAVIDSON (28) Farm Servant, Linlathen, Dundee	Cupar
	* 8. 1.80 near bridge (15)	
15.	Mrs EASTON Widow	Edinburgh
16.	Robert FOWLIS (21) Mason, Lochee, Dundee	St Fort
	* 12. 1.80 near bridge (26)	
17.	David GRAHAM (37) Teacher, Stirling	Edinburgh
18.	John HAMILTON (32) Grocer and Spirit Dealer, Dundee	Leuchars
19.	JAMES Foster HENDERSON (22) Labourer, Dundee	Ladybank
	* 8. 1.80 near 'Mars' (18)	
20.	Eliz HENDRY or MANN (62) Grandmother of Lizzie Brown, Forfar	Leuchars
21.	David JOBSON (39) Oil and Colour Merchant, Dundee	Ladybank
	* 17. 2.80 near Newport (37)	
22.	David JOHNSTON (24) Railway Guard, Edinburgh	Edinburgh
	* 5. 1.80 near bridge (2)	
23.	George JOHNSTON (25) Mechanic	St Fort
	* 8. 1.80 near bridge (21)	
24.	William JACK (23) Grocer, Dundee	Dairsie
	* 6. 1.80 near bridge (4)	
25.	Margaret KINNEAR (17) Domestic Servant, Dundee	Leuchars
	* 14. 4.80 near Abertay Lightship (44)	
26.	James LESLIE (22) Clerk, Dundee	Leuchars
	* 6. 1.80 near bridge (3)	
27.	John LAWSON (25) Plasterer, Dundee	Ladybank
	* 10. 1.80 near bridge (24)	
28.	David McBEATH (44) Railway Guard, Dundee	Edinburgh
	* 13. 1.80 near bridge (28)	
30.	William MACDONALD (41) Sawmiller, Dundee	Newburgh
	* 7. 1.80 near 'Mars' (11)	
31.	David MACDONALD (11) Schoolboy son, Dundee	Newburgh
	* 9. 1.80 near 'Mars'	
32.	David MITCHELL (37) Engine Driver, Dundee	Edinburgh
	* 1. 3.80 between Broughty Ferry and Tayport (39)	
33.	John MARSHALL (24) Stoker, Dundee	Edinburgh
	* 7. 1.80 near bridge (7)	
34.	Donald MURRAY (49) Mail Guard, Dundee	
35.	Elizabeth MILNE Dressmaker	
36.	James MURDOCH (21) Engineer, Dundee	Edinburgh
	* 6. 2.80 near bridge (33)	
37.	James MILLAR Flax Dresser, Dysart	Edinburgh
	* 7. 1.80 near 'Mars' (10)	
38.	George McINTOSH (43) Goods Guard, Dundee	Edinburgh
	* 16. 2.80 near Inverkeillor (36)	
39.	David NEISH (37) Teacher/Registrar, Lochee, Dundee	Kirkcaldy
	* 7. 1.80 near 'Mars' (12)	
40.	Bella NEISH (5) Daughter of above Lochee, Dundee	Kirkcaldy
	* 27. 1.80 Wormit Bay (32)	
41.	Walter NESS (24) Saddler, Dundee	Ladybank
	* 7. 1.80 near 'Mars' (14)	
42.	George NESS	Edinburgh
	* 13. 1.80 near bridge (29)	
43.	William NEILSON (31) Gateshead	Newburgh
44.	Mrs NICOLL (24) Dundee	
45.	James PATON (42) Mechanic, Edinburgh DID NOT TRAVEL	
46.	William PEEBLES (30/40) Broughty Ferry	
	* 9. 1.80 near 'Mars' (19)	
47.	James PEEBLES (15½) Apprentice Grocer, Newport	St Fort
	* 11. 4.80 Tayport Harbour (42)	
48.	William ROBERTSON (21) Labourer, Dundee	Abernethy
	* 27. 4.80 near 'Mars'(46)	
49.	Alexander ROBERTSON (23) Labourer, Dundee	Abernethy
	* 8. 1.80 near bridge (17)	
50.	David SCOTT (26) Goods Guard, Dundee	
51.	Robert SYME (22) Clerk, Dundee	Edinburgh
	* 11. 1.80 near bridge (25)	
52.	John SCOTT (30) Pipemaker	
	* 23. 1.80 near bridge (31)	
53.	Peter Grey SALMOND (43) Blacksmith, Dundee	Sinclairtown
	* 7. 2.80 Monifieth (35)	
54.	Anne SPENCE (21) Weaver	Newburgh
55.	Eliza SMART (22) Domestic Servant	St Fort
56.	John SHARP (35) Joiner, Dundee	
	* 7. 1.80 near 'Mars' (13)	Leuchars
57.	George TAYLOR (25) Mason, Dundee	
	* 11. 1.80 east of Tayport (40)	Newburgh
59.	William THRELFELL (18) Confectioner, Dundee	
	* 7. 1.80 near 'Mars' (9)	Edinburgh
60.	William VEITCH (18) Cabinetmaker, Dundee	
	* 13. 1.80 near bridge (27)	Cupar
61.	David WATSON, Commission Agent, Newport	
	* 7. 1.80 near bridge	
62.	Robert WATSON (34) Moulder, Dundee	
	* 6. 1.80 near 'Mars'	Cupar
63.	David WATSON (19) Son of above, Dundee	
	* 16. 1.80 east of Broughty Castle (30)	Cupar
64.	Robert WATSON (6) Brother of above, Dundee	
	* 9. 1.80 off bridge (22)	Cupar

An official list issued by the Dundee Police showing when and where the bodies were recovered, as well as a number which were never found or reported missing. The ticket count at St Fort was not entirely to be relied on.

Dr William Pole FRS, 1814–1900. A consulting
engineer with (for a practising engineer of the
period) an unusually good understanding of higher
mathematics and structural theory. He acted as Bouch's
technical adviser at the Tay Bridge Inquiry.

This was Caledonian country, and in certain minds those upstarts at Edinburgh had received their comeuppance. The Jeremiahs sadly shook their heads. They had been proven right.

Towards the end of the first day Dugald Drummond, Locomotive and Carriage Superintendent of the NBR, was closely questioned regarding the derailed carriages. Drummond was a notoriously cantankerous character with a blistering tongue, but in Court he was on his best behaviour. His main evidence would be given later when the Inquiry had adjourned to London. On this occasion he was closely questioned on the carriages and their weight and stability.

The Inquiry resumed at Dundee on 26 February 1880 and adjourned on 3 March pending a transfer of the hearing to London. A number of passengers gave evidence, along with several of the engine drivers who regularly worked across the bridge. All the drivers had been well drilled by Dugald Drummond, the Locomotive Superintendent, swearing one by one that they had never exceeded the 25mph limit which had been recommended by Major-General Hutchinson. Drummond was a hard man when crossed, and they knew what they had to say. Many of the others to be examined were the contractor's staff from the Wormit Foundry, and they told of bad management and bad practices, bad iron, and lack of competent supervision by the site engineers. There was much talk of 'Beaumont's Egg', a compound used to fill blowholes in poor castings, and of the lugs, which held the diagonal bracings of the piers, being knocked off when tested with a 4lb hammer. The moulders were a motley crew, recruited from those unable to find work in the busy Dundee foundries. They were simple men, inarticulate when questioned by the English lawyers, and overawed by their surroundings. One or two were obviously drunk, but what their evidence revealed was not reassuring. Others among them had personal axes to grind and no love for their employer.

There had been no lack of evidence that all was not well with the bridge during 1879. The ex-Provost of Dundee, proprietor of a major foundry in the city, had complained that the morning commuter train from Newport often vibrated so much that it was like being on a galloping horse, and he put this down to the trains frequently racing the Newport ferry.

William Henry Barlow. One of the great names in civil engineering in the latter half of the nineteenth century. He was a Commissioner on the 1880 Inquiry into the fall of Bouch's Tay Bridge, and later was Chief Engineer of its replacement.

His complaint to the stationmaster at Dundee produced no improvement, for that worthy considered the running of the trains to be none of his business, and he was not inclined to cross swords with Drummond. Ex-Provo Robertson became so alarmed that he went back to using the ferry. Nor would he allow his family to use the bridge. The painters working on the bridge complained of severe vibration as trains passed, to the extent that they had to secure their paint cans to prevent them being thrown off. Yet no one in authority, not even Bouch, if indeed he was informed of it, had shown any concern.

Major-General Hutchinson

On 27 January, St John Vincent Day, a patent agent at Glasgow was due to read a Paper to the Institution of Engineers and Shipbuilders in Scotland, which ostensibly was to be a critique of Bouch's design for the proposed Forth Bridge. Day had been over to Dundee on a private visit, and what he had seen there caused him to preface his remarks with a blistering attack on Bouch and the Tay Bridge. This was not universally well received as the matter was *sub judice*, and Day was taken aback by the strength of the opposition. He sought Rothery's advice and was encouraged to proceed with an open discussion in the public interest. In Day's condemnation of Bouch Rothery recognised an ally. However, Day went on to criticise General Hutchinson's examination of the bridge, and by implication the Board of Trade.

Hutchinson was instructed to report on his actions when inspecting the bridge. The obvious criticism that he had made no tests for wind effects was answered in his report:

> I was anxious to see how the lateral stiffness of the piers might be affected by the action of a high wind upon the side of a train in motion over the bridge. This I had intended to get if possible an opportunity of doing before the traffic commenced running, but I was laid aside by serious illness shortly after the inspection and before my recovery the bridge had been opened for traffic.

Colonel William Yolland CB FRS, 1810–1885. He is seen here as a young captain in the Royal Engineers. He had thirty-one years' service with the Railway Inspectorate, the last eight as Chief inspector. He died just before he was due to retire.

There is an implicit criticism of Colonel Yolland, though this was never brought up in the Court, that he could have sent another Inspector while Hutchinson was indisposed. But Yolland was one of the Commissioners!

The Inquiry Moves to London

By the tenth day of the Hearing, 19 April 1880, the Inquiry had been moved to Westminster Hall in London. It was now that the really important witnesses would be called, including Bouch himself. His evidence was vital, and to a considerable extent he condemned himself out of his own mouth. His deafness made it difficult for him, his heart was troubling him, and he was under great stress. Although in theory he was not on trial all present were in no doubt that he was fighting for his professional life. It was extraordinary that, except for poor faithful Henry Noble, there was not one person above foreman level who had been employed by Bouch to supervise the building of the bridge who appeared in Court to speak on his behalf.

In the normal course of events William Paterson, who had been employed by Bouch as resident engineer from the beginning, was the man best qualified to give an account of his stewardship. Sadly, on hearing the news at his home in Perth of the fall of the bridge, Paterson had suffered a severe paralytic stroke and was confined to his bed, his speech gone and unable to move. However, Paterson had employed a personal assistant, a Mr Ralph, also living at Perth, who had been on the bridge almost every day. Strangely Ralph was not called to give evidence, although eminently well qualified to do so. William Bouch had completed his five-year pupilage in his father's office, again mostly engaged on the bridge, but doubtless his father would not have wished him to be questioned.

For other assistance in his duties, Paterson mostly had to make do with a succession of Bouch's pupils, for Bouch, like Mr Wackford Squeers before him, believed that learning on the job was by far the best way. One of the most recently qualified pupils, Alexander C. Raff, had taken his degree at Glasgow University before obtaining his practical training on

Major-General Charles Scrope Hutchinson CB, 1826–1912. He became a Railway Inspector in 1867 and retired in 1895 after twenty-eight years service, the last three as Chief Inspector. He inspected the first Tay Bridge, but received no blame for its fall.

the bridge, and had subsequently become resident engineer on the Arbroath and Montrose line then under construction. He too was never called, nor was Bouch's personal assistant and office manager, George Trimble. It was certainly no time for Bouch's other ex-pupils to boast of where they learned their profession.

Dr William Pole (a Doctor of Music, for he was a typical Victorian polymath and a highly respected organist among other things) was by profession a consulting engineer and an unusually accomplished mathematician, and had been for eleven years Secretary of the Institution of Civil Engineers. On this occasion he was acting as an independent technical adviser to Bouch, and his evidence would carry some weight. As a result it occupied most of the twenty-second and twenty-third days of the Inquiry.

The questioning concerned mainly the matter of wind pressures. It was established on the basis of Smeaton's experiments a century earlier, and advice given to Bouch by the Astronomer Royal, Sir George Airy. Airy was a highly accomplished mathematician but also interested in solving practical engineering problems. He had advised Bouch regarding wind pressures on the proposed Forth Bridge, but unfortunately this information did not reach Stewart in time. In 1873, the allowance of 20psf made by Allan Stewart in his calculations was entirely adequate, based on Smeaton's experiments and this was something of which Bouch must have known and approved. Any excess allowance would have been 'special'. It was also established that some 34psi would have been needed for the piers to blow over sideways, even without holding down bolts. Moreover, the lightest of the carriages would have been blown over at about 33psf.

Components of the bridge were submitted by Henry Law for testing at David Kirkaldy's testing works in London. Kirkaldy's report that the lugs under test failed at about one third of their theoretical strength was considered without arriving at, or even seeking, any explanation. Henry Law had handled the testing programme very badly, and what might have been vital evidence was passed over. Law also failed to publish Kirkaldy's full report. Pole expressed his opinion that the impact of the two derailed carriages might have been the final straw for the overstressed lugs. This offered little comfort for Bouch, for a bridge that had been allowed to reach such a parlous state was doomed sooner or later.

Allan Duncan Stewart, a Cambridge graduate of great mathematical ability. He acted as structural consultant to Bouch for about twenty-five years, and his work on the Tay Bridge was praised. He later became Chief Assistant to Benjamin Baker.

Allan Duncan Stewart, the mathematician who calculated the various stresses on the girders and piers, was not questioned regarding the girders, as it was common ground that they were very well designed and more than adequate for their duty. In fact General Hutchinson had taken the unusual step of testing the girders with a 50% overload. The diagonal ties between the two tripods of each pier were considered in detail although there was no firm evidence that any tie had failed, and in Kirkaldy's testing machine they had shown the iron to be of reasonable quality though not always quite reaching the 21 tons breaking load demanded by the specification. What did emerge from the questioning was that the ties under 20psf wind load would have been stressed to 6¾tsi or 50% more than Stewart had designed for, thus reducing the factor of safety from 4 to 2.67.

After the Inquiry finished Stewart was taken to task for this by Barlow and Yolland, but kept his own counsel – had Bouch agreed to this minor economy as he did with the lug bolts?

Strangely, none of the lawyers, who may not have fully understood the implications, nor did the engineers, who knew very well the error, chose to press Stewart on this anomaly. The design called for ties of ¾in thickness while those found in the bridge were only ½in. Had the contractors, who were under severe financial pressures, cut the thickness to save a few hundred pounds? It will never be known. The ½in iron held in a ⁷/₈in slot in the lug could have caused the bolts to bend, as they were observed to have done, and burst apart the lugs. This is something of which Bouch could have had no knowledge. Since it appeared that no harm had been done the matter was given no further consideration, yet the highly eccentric loading presents a very plausible reason for the failure of the lugs under a load which they could have resisted with a straight pull. This might have been revealed in Kirkaldy's notes on his tests had they not been destroyed by Second World War bombing.

The renowned Benjamin Baker (who a few years later would design the Forth Bridge with Allan Stewart as his chief assistant) was questioned on wind forces. He expressed his opinion that the highest pressure on the Tay Bridge during the storm had not exceeded 15psf, and he further stated that he himself designed for 28psf. He could offer no explanation for the premature failure of the lugs while under test, and he was positive that the lugs had not failed under wind pressure alone. His opinion was that a degree of shock loading in addition could have led to the breakages, and that this might well have arisen from the impact of the two derailed carriages.

Sir William Arrol, the great Scottish bridge builder. He was awarded the contract for Bouch's Queensferry bridge, but this was cancelled in 1880. Later he built the present Forth Bridge for Fowler and Baker, the largest bridge in the UK.

There was evidence, though it was never brought to the attention of the Inquiry, that on the fatal night wind conditions in the Tay Valley had been affected by cyclonic action, which would produce very high wind pressures over a narrow front. An eye witness claimed to have seen waterspouts in the river, and a more reliable witness told of damage to a farm near Cupar. The wind there had done much destruction to a farm steading, even to the extent of stripping the lead off a flat roof, rolling it up and depositing it some distance away. A farm only a quarter of a mile away was untouched. In 1824 the bridge at Montrose had been destroyed in a similar storm. None of this would have saved Bouch, but it does suggest that the bridge may have suffered greater wind forces than the Inquiry was led to believe.

Edgar Gilkes, managing partner of Hopkins, Gilkes & Co., the contractors, was unprepared to admit to any of the alleged deficiencies in the foundry or elsewhere as reported by earlier witnesses. He denied that the conical holes in the lugs could have endangered the bridge. He too supported the hypothesis that a combination of tension and shock had caused the lugs to fail. All in all he expressed the view that both material and workmanship had been of a high quality in accordance with the specification, and that the work had been properly supervised by his staff, as well as by himself on his irregular visits to Dundee. This completed the examination of witnesses.

Sir Thomas Bouch is Questioned

On the nineteenth day of the Inquiry and after some preliminary skirmishing by the lawyers, Bouch took the witness stand and was sworn in. There had been talk that Bouch had lost his mind and was unfit for questioning. When he entered the witness box he looked, to those in Court, a man old beyond his fifty-eight years, his grey beard streaked with white. His deafness made it difficult for him to follow the proceedings. It was an Inquiry and not an Inquisition, and the questioning by all the lawyers showed some sympathy for the predicament in which Bouch found himself. The Court was unusually subdued as Mr Bidder questioned Bouch on his previous experience. With some excusable pride Bouch replied that he had built a great number of bridges.

John Walker was one of the great railway General Managers and was allowed much freedom of action by the NBR Directors. He served the NBR for twenty-five years and was a personal friend of Bouch, a trustee of Bouch's will and a pallbearer at his funeral.

'I do not suppose anybody has built more.' Bidder started the questioning by leading his client at length through the history of the bridge and its construction and subsequent maintenance up to the time of the accident. Nothing of great consequence emerged until Question 16798:

Will you give to the Court your opinion as to what did cause the accident that destroyed the Tay Bridge?

Bouch: Well, I have thought a great deal about it very anxiously and my own opinion is fixed now; that it was caused by the capsizing of one of the last or the two last carriages – that is to say, the second class carriage and the van; that they canted over against the girder.

The explanation that Bouch put before the Court was a very simple one. There was evidence, such as severe damage to the track, that the last two carriages had become derailed somewhere around the middle of the fourth girder and had canted over, and Bouch argued that this had damaged some of the side bracing of the eastern girder. The coupling between the train and the fifth carriage had broken, and the frames of both carriages had partly telescoped against the end of the fourth girder. Such was the shock, argued Bouch, that no bridge could have been expected to stand it in addition to the fury of the storm. Nonetheless, the bridge should have been of adequate strength to withstand such abuse. On the other hand, if the bridge had been progressively weakened by the racking of the piers in previous gales, which appeared to be the case in spite of (or perhaps because of) Henry Noble's valiant efforts, the impact of the carriages might have triggered a collapse. No one but Bouch himself took his argument seriously.

Then followed Mr Trayner's examination of Bouch on behalf of the Board of Trade, but this disclosed nothing of special importance. By this time in the afternoon Bouch had been giving evidence all day and was visibly tiring, and the Court adjourned until the following Monday, 3 May, when Bouch would be recalled to face further questioning. On Monday morning, right at the beginning, he made a bad start. Asked if in designing the bridge he had made any allowance at all for wind pressure, he replied, 'Not specially'.

There was a sudden silence, then a murmur ran round the courtroom. Thinking that perhaps Bouch had misheard the question, Rothery repeated it and received the same reply. It is difficult to understand why Bidder failed to intervene on his client's behalf, for Bouch's answer had been ambiguous. Had he meant that he had taken the normal precautions but had not felt it necessary to go to exceptional lengths? That will never be known. *The Engineer*, when publishing a leading article on 9 July 1880, took it upon itself to report Bouch's answer as 'made no allowance whatever' which was a great injustice, though by then it was too late to do further damage to Bouch's reputation.

It had been pointed out previously that on 5 October 1869 Bouch had written to Colonel Yolland, asking if it was necessary to take the force of the wind into account. Yolland had replied three days later that, 'we do not take the force of the wind into account when open lattice girders are used for spans not exceeding 200ft.' Furthermore, Bouch must surely have known that Allan Stewart had designed for 20psf wind pressure.

Trayner turned to the cause of the accident. At one point things became heated when Bouch was accused of failing to answer and this time Bidder had to intervene. Mr Rothery, the Wreck Commissioner, sought to question Bouch, but looking at the man before him, fighting for his professional life, even Rothery could not suppress a twinge of sympathy, though later he would destroy him without compunction:

> I must ask you some questions, and I will endeavour to put them in such a way that they shall not in any way distress you, for we all have a feeling for you under the circumstances; but you can quite understand that it is our duty to ascertain the cause of this casualty, and nobody, perhaps, has a greater interest in that cause being ascertained than you yourself.

The questioning that followed was inconclusive except that a vital point was raised concerning the substitution of $1\frac{1}{8}$in bolts in the lugs for the $1\frac{1}{2}$in bolts originally specified. Bouch stated that he had no recollection of the alteration. Elsewhere he confessed that it had been done at the instigation of Albert Groethe, the Contractor's Site Manager, as an economy measure, and that it had been done with his approval but that he had not expected the bolts to bend. This bending may well have contributed to the premature failure of so many of the lugs. Bouch was then allowed to stand down. After answering 820 questions over two days his ordeal was not yet over, for he was briefly recalled the following morning.

Some public-spirited whistleblower had seen fit to inform the Board of Trade that Bouch was a substantial shareholder in the firm of Hopkins, Gilkes & Co., contractors for the Tay Bridge. Bidder explained the circumstances. When the contract was let in 1874 Bouch had no interest whatever in the firm except that he had known them at the Belah and Deepdale viaducts as efficient and reliable contractors. On the death of his brother William in 1876, Bouch inherited about £35,000 worth of shares in the Company and a further liability for calls of £13,000 more. When the Company was in financial difficulties and had to be restructured, Bouch was obliged to find that £13,000 to pay off part of the firm's liabilities to their Bankers.

Instructed by the Board of Trade, Mr Trayner did not wish to pursue the matter further, but Rothery thought that Bouch should have a chance to speak. Under questioning from Bidder, Bouch confirmed the facts as already stated and was allowed to withdraw. As an engineer his credentials might be open to question, but his personal integrity remained unchallenged. In fact, throughout the questioning the former country publican's son had behaved as a gentleman should. He made no attempt to implicate others as many lesser men would have done, and was ready to take the full blame on his own shoulders.

Now came Bidder's turn to discuss the evidence on behalf of his client, Sir Thomas Bouch. He freely accepted that Bouch was accountable for all aspects of the work and confirmed that his client had no desire to evade his responsibilities. Much of his argument concerned wind force, and he raised a query concerning the figures quoted by the Astronomer Royal, suggesting that the actual wind pressure was as much as 40psf. He attributed the fall of the bridge to failure of the lugs from the impact of the two derailed carriages added to the wind, and hinted that the excessive wind might be regarded as an Act of God which would exonerate his client – in all Bidder's report occupies twenty-eight pages.

Mr Trayner, speaking on behalf of the Board of Trade, discussed the design of the bridge and accepted that it was not an inherently bad design but that it could have been bettered. He conceded that Hopkins, Gilkes & Co. had built the bridge to the best of their ability, but that this did not exempt them from blame for the various deficiencies shown up by the evidence. With regard to the inspection by General Hutchinson, he was of the opinion that the General had done all that could reasonably have been expected of him, bearing in mind his limited powers. He was critical of Sir Thomas Bouch for failing to exercise proper personal supervision during construction and during the maintenance period, when the world's longest iron bridge was left in the charge of Henry Noble, a most careful and conscientious inspector of brickwork but ignorant of iron structures. To conclude he set about demolishing the case that derailment of the last two carriages had caused the fall of the bridge. All this he managed to cover in eight pages.

Mr Webster spoke on behalf of the contractors, mainly to refute some of the criticisms which had been levelled against them. He too conceded that the fall of the bridge had been precipitated by the impact of the derailed carriages, but disputed that any defects in the structure had contributed to this. This completed the Inquiry at the end of its twenty-fifth day. All that now remained to be done was for the Commissioners to submit their report. Ideally this should have been unanimous, and Rothery took it upon himself to write what purported to be a unanimous report, but since there were serious differences of opinion between Mr Rothery and the engineers, the latter insisted on submitting their majority report and the Commissioner of Wrecks reluctantly submitted his own minority report but refused to change the wording.

The Majority Report by Messrs Barlow and Yolland

In view of the complexity and the volume of evidence presented to the Inquiry the report by the two engineers was fairly short at twelve pages. After a general survey of the construction of the bridge, they concentrated on the diagonal bracing, and the cast-iron lugs were considered to be the cause of the failure. The tie bars are shown to be undersized and therefore would become overloaded at the design wind pressure of 20psf. Since there was no reported failure of any of the tie bars this matter is again given no further consideration. The hypothesis that the bridge was destroyed by the derailment of the two rear carriages is completely dismissed and Bouch's defence is discredited. Their conclusions were that the piers were of insufficient strength and that much of the workmanship was unsatisfactory. Supervision was inadequate and someone with greater knowledge than Noble should have attended to the maintenance. They recommend to the Board of Trade an urgent investigation into the effects of wind pressure. Importantly, no attempt was made to apportion blame, since they did not consider this a function of the Inquiry. In this they were perfectly correct and Rothery far exceeded his remit.

Rothery's Minority Report

Henry Rothery thought differently, and prepared a lengthy report written in the first person plural, which gave the impression that it was the unanimous report of all three Commissioners. Barlow and Yolland were furious, and refused to sign it, and demanded that it should be rewritten in the singular as Rothery's own personal report. This he refused to do, but grudgingly agreed to incorporate an addition at the end outlining the differences between the engineers and himself. As far as the public was concerned Rothery's remained the definitive report. Omitting the introductory description of the bridge, it was printed in full in *The Engineer* and serialised over four weekly issues.

Rothery had no doubts as to whom to blame for the fall of the bridge. The North British Railway Company was criticised for failing to supervise the maintenance during the period when it was delegated to Bouch for the generous sum of £105 pa. In addition, they had failed to ensure that trains did not exceed the 25mph limit recommended (not imposed for he had no power to do that) by General Hutchinson. Hopkins, Gilkes & Co. were held to blame for the malpractices in the Wormit foundry. It was agreed that General Hutchinson had done all that could be expected of him when inspecting the bridge, but he could possibly be faulted for not considering the effects of wind pressure. He had in fact reported that he would have liked to have seen how the bridge behaved in a high wind, but due to illness this further inspection was never made. Though it was not mentioned, Yolland could have sent another Inspector to make this vital check. When it came to the part played by Sir Thomas Bouch, Rothery did not pull his punches:

> The conclusion, then, to which we have come, is that this bridge was badly designed, badly constructed, and badly maintained, and that its downfall was due to inherent defects in the structure, which must sooner or later have brought it down. For these defects, both in the design, the construction, and the maintenance, Sir Thomas Bouch is, in our opinion, mainly to blame. For the faults of design he is entirely responsible. For those of construction he is principally to blame in not having exercised that supervision over the work which would have enabled him to detect and apply a remedy to them. And for the faults of maintenance he is also principally, if not entirely, to blame in having neglected to maintain an inspection over the structure, as its character imperatively demanded.

A cruel and damning indictment by any standards, but one which met with general public approval. Rothery had delivered to Joseph Chamberlain, President of the Board of Trade, the head of Sir Thomas Bouch on a charger. But had justice been done or did it merely appear to have been done? Rothery had performed his duty well and was widely praised for his uncompromising stance. Barlow and Yolland were dismissed as pusillanimous if they protested, and they wisely kept their heads down. A number of engineers were jockeying to replace Bouch as designer of the new Tay Bridge, Barlow among them, and Yolland still had to face Joseph Chamberlain and explain why he had failed to make a second inspection of the original bridge during a high wind as General Hutchinson had favoured.

There were some who thought that Bouch had been badly treated and that Rothery should have toned down his report, One who protested was A.J. Dickson, Bouch's solicitor, who wrote to Adam Johnstone, chief solicitor of the NBR:

> What an unmerciful report this is that has emanated from the Court of Inquiry. It seems too severe in every way to be just… This report magnifies and rides to death (particularly the Wreck Commissioner's) every fault that can be picked and makes little allowance for the judgement of others and the possible imperfections, ignorance, or absence of unbiased vision on the part of the Reporters themselves in a matter which could in all essential parts remain a mystery until the end of all things.

In addition A.J. Dickson, Bouch's solicitor, wrote to Barlow and Yolland complaining that Rothery had passed off his individual report as being a unanimous one. Their reply came swiftly: 'Mr Rothery was not warranted in representing our opinions as concurrent with his own in matters not referred to in our report.' Sadly, the damage had already been done and this was cold comfort to Bouch.

The Last Months of Sir Thomas Bouch

There is ample evidence that Bouch was devastated when faced with the ruins of his bridge. It had brought him fame, fortune, and honour from a grateful Sovereign. Now Bouch found himself in a state of denial – nothing he had done could have brought down his bridge, and his first duty was to see it rebuilt even better than before, of course this time with a double track. The senior officers of the NBR were of much the same mind when they met on the day after the fall. Their considered opinion was that the bridge should be rebuilt as soon as possible and that Bouch should be in charge. This was confirmed at a meeting of the Directors in Edinburgh, though there were misgivings about Bouch's part in the new design. In this they were firmly supported by the Dundee papers. It was further decided that work on the Forth Bridge should cease and that Arrol should be informed accordingly. Public attitudes towards bridging the Tay had completely changed. Before it had been built the doubters feared that the bridge would be an expensive white elephant, if indeed it could ever be built. Now a bridge was regarded as indispensable, but meanwhile the redundant wagon ferries came out of retirement and were returned to service.

During January 1880 Bouch carried on his work almost as if nothing had happened though he could not disguise his personal distress. There was much work already on hand. The Arbroath & Montrose Railway was proceeding, and there was a lengthy iron bridge to be built over the river South Esk. The Forth Bridge Act had been passed as far back as 1874, and in due course the contract let to William Arrol who had started building a brickworks at North Queensferry, and preparing an erecting ground at Dalmeny on the south bank. A Parliamentary survey and Bill for the Edinburgh South Side and Suburban Junction Railway was in hand. To this was now added the new design for the Tay Bridge. However, January did not pass smoothly.

Although Bouch was pressing ahead with his plans for rebuilding the Tay Bridge, his relationship with the NBR was rapidly becoming untenable. The Directors had known Bouch for thirty years, and many had become personal friends, and the thought of dispensing with his services after so many years was distasteful and embarrassing. It would probably fall to the Chairman, John Stirling, to break the news. Whatever their personal feelings, the lawyers were more pragmatic. It was abundantly clear that no Bill for a new bridge would pass Parliamentary scrutiny with Bouch's name attached. He had his new plans prepared, but Adam Johnstone wrote to explain the situation.

When the Bill did come up for consideration it was strongly attacked by a Mr Anderson, who was believed to be in the pay of the NBR's implacable opponent, the Caledonian Railway. Anderson did not mince his words:

> This House has now to consider whether under these circumstances they ought to allow the very parties who are to blame to come to the House, in the last month of the session, and endeavour to rush through Parliament a Bill not for the construction of a new bridge under the supervision of new engineers, but a Bill for the patching up of the miserable old structure. I myself have seen the plans and specifications, and they bear the name of Sir Thomas Bouch. Instead of coming to the House for a Bill I think that some of the parties might rather be standing in a criminal dock to answer for their negligence.

For the sake of appearances, Chamberlain thought it proper to shed a few crocodile tears for Bouch, and he completed his statement with the following words:

> At the present moment there is no one more deserving of pity than the civil engineer who designed and constructed the Tay Bridge and who, as the law now stands, is held responsible for its defects. With this case in view it in the highest degree improbable that any civil engineer entrusted with a similar task in future will commit similar errors.

Nor of course would any Railway Inspector in future.

Despite this, the Bill received a second reading, but Bouch had to be thrown to the sharks. James Brunlees was appointed as the new engineer by the Board, and Johnstone wrote to Bouch with the news, leaving Bouch with no option but to resign. Since he was still engineer to the Forth Bridge enterprise, the NBR also applied for a Forth Bridge Abandonment Bill which was granted. Willam Arrol's contract was swiftly terminated and compensation paid. Although all this had struck Bouch a deadly blow, he still had work to finish though no longer with the support of the Directors of the North British Railway, still less the public.

This was not to be an end to the matter, for the performance of General Hutchinson was raised first by St John Vincent Day at a meeting of the Institution of Engineers and Shipbuilders in Scotland at a meeting held in Glasgow, where he criticised General Hutchinson's inspection of the bridge in 1878. Eventually the matter was raised on the floor of the House of Commons to the fury of Joseph Chamberlain. Chamberlain sprang to the defence of the Board of Trade and its Railway Inspecting Officers with a report to both Houses of Parliament. At the Inquiry it had been accepted that Hutchinson had carried out very thorough load tests, and beyond that he could only make a superficial examination of the completed work. He could not be held to blame if the 25mph maximum speed which he recommended was exceeded as he had no power to enforce it. It was the responsibility of the NBR to see that it was observed.

There is an implicit criticism of Colonel Yolland, though this was never brought up in the Court of Inquiry, that he could have sent another Inspector while Hutchinson was indisposed. But Yolland was one of the Commissioners!

To quote from Chamberlain's report. First pointing out that The Board of Trade had no authority to supervise the maintenance of the bridge once it had been opened for traffic he continued:

> Under these circumstances it is clear that Major-General Hutchinson could not be responsible for any defects in the Tay Bridge which were not discoverable in such an inspection as he was empowered to make. It is clear that he cannot be held responsible for faults in the material and workmanship which were not visible when the work was completed and painted, still less for defects which did not exist until after his inspection. As regards design, it may be held that he ought to have seen that the work was essentially weak and to have reported accordingly, but that is, to say the least, doubtful. The duty of an inspecting officer, so far as regards design, is to see that the construction is not such as to transgress those rules and precautions which practice and experience had proved to be necessary for safety. If he were to go beyond this, or if he were to make himself responsible for every novel design, and if he were to attempt to introduce new rules and practices not accepted by the profession he would be removing from the civil engineer and taking upon himself a responsibility not committed to him by parliament.

This was restating the understood position which had existed since the failure of Stephenson's Dee Bridge in 1847. There, Major-General Pasley had examined the bridge as closely as he was able and could not be blamed for fundamental design errors. Even less could General Pasley be held responsible for Stephenson's reckless action in ordering many tons of ballast to be dumped on the bridge many months after the inspection. In the final analysis the responsibility lay on the engineer and his employers, and that was how the position remained in 1880.

Although perhaps overshadowed by two other long-serving Inspectors – Colonel Yolland CB FRS (1810-85) with thirty-one years service when he died in office just before he was due to retire, and the indefatigable Captain Sir Henry Tyler KCB (1827-1908) who accumulated twenty-four years service before becoming Chairman of the

Westinghouse Brake Co. and a Member of Parliament for twelve years – Major-General Hutchinson CB (1826-1912) served for twenty-eight years, and inspected the Forth Bridge every quarter while under construction. Of him it was said:

> He had a passion for work, in the execution of which he displayed a zeal amounting to enthusiasm. He never spared himself, and often after a comfortless night journey on cross-country trains, he would snatch a hurried breakfast at some dreary railway buffet, and begin a long day's work of inspection at eight o'clock in the morning, much to the surprise and not always the joy of the railway officers, who wondered how in the world he got there. He gained the warm friendship and respect not only of his colleagues, but all the officers of the railways of the United Kingdom with whom he was brought into contact in the course of his official duties.

One major effect of the fall of the Tay Bridge, in which wind forces had played a significant part, was to concentrate the minds of both practising engineers and academics on design of structures to resist the wind, and also to measure wind pressures accurately, which proved to be a very inexact science. For many years much was left to the judgment of the individual engineer responsible, and their estimates varied widely. Britain also has a number of hurricanes every year which are highly destructive over a narrow area, but cannot be compared with a tropical hurricane. The Tay Estuary has a history of such hurricanes, including one which destroyed the bridge at Montrose in 1824. There was a reliable report of a hurricane at Cupar, a few miles west of the bridge, on the night of 28 December 1879. Could this have been the last straw for the bridge?

The vultures were circling. Henry Law had been visited by Johnstone as far back as 14 June to discuss the rebuilding, and was left firmly under the impression that it was he who would undertake the work. Groethe wrote offering his own plans, and referring to Bouch's plans he commented 'It is as nasty a work that I for one would not like to undertake it in contract'. His own part in Bouch's downfall was overlooked. Another engineer who had done some work for the NBR was W.R. Galbraith, and on 10 July he wrote to John Stirling offering his services.

W.H. Barlow already had a foot firmly in the door. Back in April Hopkins, Gilkes & Co. had ceased trading, and were metamorphosed into The Teesside Ironworks & Tees Engine Co. which, in one form or another, survived until the nationalisation of steel.

13

THE SWANSONG OF
SIR THOMAS BOUCH

The long drawn-out Inquiry into the fall of the Tay Bridge was an ordeal for which Sir Thomas Bouch could not have been prepared. The previous year had been a busy one, with the final preparations for his even greater bridge over the Forth at Queensferry underway. His bridge at Dundee had been widely praised, though the Jeremiahs pointed to its slim girders and spindly piers and prophesied its doom one stormy night. Bouch had given Scotland the world's longest bridge over tidal waters, and though often derided as a country cousin by the great names of the civil engineering profession, secure in their Westminster enclave, Bouch, for a few months, was riding high. When Queen Victoria graciously agreed that her train south from Ballater should leave its familiar Caledonian highway and follow the devious route to Dundee and the Tay Bridge, plain Thomas Bouch rode on the locomotive footplate while the Royal Train was on North British rails. The knighthood which was bestowed upon him at Windsor a few days later completed his triumph and delighted his wife.

But, as Queen Victoria's roundabout journey over the Tay Bridge had shown, the North British Railway was still far from attaining its ultimate ambition, never in fact to be more than a dream, of possessing its own through route to Aberdeen, thus offering an independent East Coast Route northwards all the way from Berwick. Leaving aside the inconvenience and discomfort of the ferry crossing from Granton to Burntisland in Fife, which Thomas Bouch was already set to remedy, North British passengers to Aberdeen and the north-east of Scotland, on reaching Arbroath over the joint Dundee & Arbroath line, were handed over to the tender mercies of the Caledonian to complete their journeys. As a first step in achieving their ambitions the North British had watched from the sidelines the development of the little Montrose & Bervie Railway, opened in November 1865. From the first there were hopes that this would ultimately be extended north through Stonehaven to Aberdeen, thus bypassing the Caledonian entirely. Although in the beginning projected as a minor branch, and fated to remain as such, it was built as a single line but to main line standards in accordance with its potential future prospects. For many years it was dominated by the Caledonian until eventually acquired by the NBR in October 1881. By this time the Tay Bridge was down and the NBR were left with a white elephant and as such it would remain until its closure in 1951.

When Bouch had been stripped by the NBR of his responsibilities for bridging the Tay and Forth estuaries, there remained the Arbroath & Montrose Railway which was still in the course of construction. It would seem that Bouch was left with this as a kind of consolation prize, in the expectation that no great harm could result. After the opening of the first Tay Bridge, the immediate problem for the NBR was completion of the line filling the 16-mile gap between Arbroath and Montrose. This would mean that the NBR would no longer be obliged to hand over its Aberdeen passengers and freight to the Caledonian at Arbroath. Even after completion of its own line through to Montrose the NBR would still be obliged to hand over its traffic to the opposition at Kinnaber Junction, just north of Montrose.

Between Arbroath and Montrose there were no great physical obstacles except for the broad estuary of the South Esk on the approach to Montrose. With an eye to the future and overwhelming local support a prospectus was issued as early as September 1871, even before work on the Tay Bridge had started. Progress was slow. Looking ahead, the single line was to be built to main line standards with all bridges except the two Esk viaducts to be constructed for double line. After the completion of the Tay Bridge the need for the direct connection to Montrose became increasingly urgent, but Bouch was preoccupied with his new Forth Bridge, and delegated, in his usual fashion, most of the work to his resident engineer, Alexander C. Raff. Raff had been college trained in Glasgow, and while a pupil in Bouch's office he had been sent like the rest to cut his teeth at the Tay Bridge.

The only other important commission which Bouch was left with after the Inquiry was to survey the planned Edinburgh Suburban & Southside Junction Railway. This was intended to offer a local service to those citizens living in the salubrious southern suburbs of the city, but perhaps was more important to serve as a bypass to allow east-west traffic to avoid the bottle-necks through Waverley and Haymarket stations in the city centre. The introduction of horse tramways in 1871, with which Bouch was also associated, was a foretaste of the effects of the extension of rope traction to the south side towards the end of the century, and this latter service did much to attract passenger traffic away from the circuitous suburban railway. That, however, still lay in the future. Bouch was engaged on the survey for the ESSJR during 1879 and probably earlier, and the Act was passed in August 1880, nine weeks before Bouch's death. This was to be his last completed work, though the route was subsequently modified by a second Act of Parliament in 1882.

At Montrose there remained much work outstanding. During the first half of 1880, when Bouch was occupied with the Tay Bridge Inquiry, Alexander Raff was left very much to his own devices and suffered the usual problems with landowners and contractors, though 'Paddy' Waddell, the main contractor, was generally to be relied upon. The same could not always be said of some of his staff when Waddell's back was turned. He had established a good reputation at the Tay Bridge and elsewhere, and had been awarded the contract for much of the work other than the steelwork on the Forth Bridge. The troubles lay elsewhere. A contractor from Montrose for one of the iron bridges put his rivets at 4in instead of 3in centres, substantially weakening the structure. Bricks delivered to the site of one bridge were condemned as unfit for use and ordered to be removed. Shortly after the same bricks appeared on another site and were again rejected. But perhaps the greatest cross which Raff had to bear was the presence of young William Bouch who, although nominally under Raff's supervision, had been appointed by his father to be resident engineer on the iron viaduct over the main channel of the South Esk just outside Montrose.

William had started as a pupil in his father's office at the age of fifteen, which suggests that his general education had been somewhat curtailed. There was to be little college book learning for him as he followed in his father's footsteps. Like all Bouch's pupils and young assistants at the time, he would have gained much of his experience on the Tay Bridge, for apart from pupils and foremen inspectors the elderly William Paterson, resident engineer there, received little support. His personal assistant, Ralph, another Perth man, he chose and paid out of his own salary. In practice it was Gilkes' engineers who provided the skilled supervision, such as it was, but none of them were experienced in foundry work.

PROSPECTUS
OF THE
NORTH BRITISH ARBROATH AND MONTROSE RAILWAY.

Authorised Capital £170,580, in 17,058 Shares of £10 each.

*Deposit, £1 per Share on application, and £1 per Share on Allotment.
Calls of £1 per Share as required during the progress of the Works.
Interest at 5 per cent. per annum allowed on Calls paid in advance.*

Directors.

HERCULES SCOTT, Esquire of Brotherton, Chairman of the Montrose and Bervie
Railway Company.

FRANCIS ABERDEIN, Esquire of Keithock, Director of the Deeside Railway
Company.

JAMES COX, Esquire, Merchant, Dundee,   } Directors of the North
GEORGE HARRISON, Esquire, Merchant, Edinburgh, } British Railway Coy.

GEORGE ROBERTSON, Esquire, W.S., Edinburgh,   } Ex-Directors of the North
JOHN RONALD, Esquire, S.S.C., Edinburgh,   } British Railway Coy.

WILLIAM MITCHELL, Esquire, Merchant, Montrose.

Bankers.

THE NORTH OF SCOTLAND BANKING COMPANY, Aberdeen, Montrose, and Branches.
THE CITY OF GLASGOW BANK, Edinburgh, Glasgow, Dundee, and Branches.
THE NATIONAL BANK OF SCOTLAND, 37 Nicholas Lane, London, E.C.

Engineer.

THOMAS BOUCH, Esquire, C.E., Edinburgh.

Secretary.

JOHN WALKER, Secretary to the North British Railway Company, Edinburgh.

Offices.

4 PRINCES STREET, EDINBURGH.

In addition to the facilities and running powers over all or any part or parts of the Scottish North-Eastern Railway granted to the North British Company upon that Railway being amalgamated with the Caledonian Company in 1866, Parliament made special provision for securing to the North British Company the use and joint management of the Dundee and Arbroath Line, and at the same time conferred on that Company the right to apply, within the following five sessions, for power to extend their system from Arbroath northwards *via* Montrose as far as Aberdeen, and restrained the Caledonian Company from opposing such application, except as regards junctions with that line.

With the view of realising the advantages of that provision an independent Company was incorporated by an Act passed in last session of Parliament for the construction of a line from Arbroath to Montrose, to secure, in the interest of the North British Company, that important link in the chain of direct Railway communication by the East Coast between the Tay Bridge at Dundee and Aberdeen.

Prospectus of the North British Arbroath and Montrose Railway, 1871

Prospectus of the Arbroath & Montrose Railway, issued in 1871, with Thomas Bouch as engineer. This was somewhat premature, and problems culminating in the need to rebuild the South Esk Viaduct delayed until after Bouch's death.

Wormit Station about 1890 after completion of the second Tay Bridge. The small house to the right of the picture is said to have been where Bouch stayed when visiting the first bridge.

Contractor's train on Bouch's viaduct over the South Esk at Montrose. This was condemned by Colonel Yolland, Chief Inspector of Railways, and never carried a passenger train. Goods trains were allowed to cross at walking speed.

What aptitude William had for the profession his father chose for him appears to have been slight, for he never made his mark as a civil engineer in the years following his father's death. On the Montrose Viaduct the contractors were familiar faces under a different name.

Hopkins, Gilkes & Co. had been forced into restructuring as early as 1877, with the Tay Bridge still uncompleted, and in April 1880 the erstwhile partnership had metamorphosed into the Teesside Iron & Engine Works Co. Ltd. Despite this reincarnation the management remained under the direction of Edgar Gilkes, Bouch's friend for the past twenty-five years. Just what part Edgar Gilkes had played in the fall of the Tay Bridge is difficult to assess but it was not inconsiderable, and he was most fortunate to have escaped so lightly. Bouch was no mere scapegoat and deserved much of the condemnation which was heaped upon him, but Edgar Gilkes too had a great deal to answer for. In the construction of the South Esk Viaduct he did nothing to redeem himself or his company. The team at Dundee had broken up. Groethe went off to Spain, and Beattie had already left a year earlier. Camphuis went back to Holland, and one of the Delpratt brothers emigrated to Australia, where in due course he founded the South Australian steel industry. The men that Gilkes sent to Montrose were simply incompetent and William Bouch too inexperienced to control them. William certainly enjoyed his new-found freedom far from his father's eye, and drove his pony and trap around Montrose and the surrounding countryside convinced of his own importance. Raff had other views, and William wrote to his father complaining that Raff would not allow him to take levels although he felt quite competent to do so. From time to time he wrote to his father asking for funds to be provided by Raff. Not large sums, £10 or so, which went a long way then.

Work started on the iron viaduct over the main branch of the South Esk in the early months of 1878, and by 13 August Bouch reported to the Directors that 'the ironwork for the viaduct is in a forward state of erection', for so Raff told him. Five months later, in January 1879, Raff was able to report: 'eight piers completed, five sets of girders had been erected, and both abutments were complete.' Rumours started to circulate that all was not well, and in May 1879 Bouch asked for a further report from Raff. On the 17th Raff wrote, stating that many of the piles were out of line, and others up to 10ins off plumb. Piles for the raking columns, supporting the piers each side, were so out of position that the columns would not fit. At that date only Piers 21-24 at the Montrose end of the bridge were being erected. Piers 25-29 were already completed using screw piles, and these were giving no cause for concern. Raff wanted the faulty piles drawn and re-driven correctly.

Bouch was stung into action, and made one of his rare site visits. What passed between father and son will never be known, but it seems to have had little effect. To be fair to William, he was barely twenty-one, and lacked authority. His father and Edgar Gilkes had been friends since the days of the Belah and Deepdale viaducts, where Gilkes, Wilson & Co. had done an excellent job twenty years before. Things did not proceed smoothly. By July 1879, with the erection of the girders nearly completed, it was discovered that the bridge was 4ft shorter than the distance between the abutments. Once again Raff was called on to iron things out. He attributed part of the problem to the piers being out of position, and as Colonel Yolland was later to report, what should have been a straight bridge was distinctly curved. The remaining 2ft 3ins was blamed on the abutments being built too far apart. 'This is rather an awkwardness', admitted Gilkes, but, being a practical man, he cut a pair of girders through the centre, and inserted a 4ft patch.

There were other awkwardness's too. Several of the piers on timber piles showed signs of sinking under the weight of the structure alone. Bouch had 5ft-diameter cylinders cast and fitted around the piers, and sunk into the river bed, then filled with concrete. For the time being the sinking ceased. By the end of August 1879, the ironwork of the viaduct was almost complete, and Waddell was set to finish the painting. Raff recommended to Bouch that the girders should be grey, over a white undercoat, with brown or black for the piers. The line was about ready for a Board of Trade inspection by the end of 1879, but the fall of the Tay Bridge threw the project into complete disarray. The traffic which should have come over the Tay Bridge was reduced to a trickle, since the resurrected wagon ferry service between Tayport and Broughty Ferry could not handle anything like the volume which had built up since the opening of the Tay Bridge in 1878.

While, prior to the fall of the Tay Bridge, Bouch had been riding on the crest of a wave of public esteem, overnight he was vilified, and called a murderer in the streets, for some seventy-five lives were believed to have been lost. Moreover, public faith in iron bridges and their engineers had been shattered. The Esk Viaduct was an embarrassment to the North British, fighting off criticism of their part in the Tay Bridge affair. For months it stood unused and unloved.

The Court of Inquiry into the Tay Bridge published its findings in early July 1880. It was the minority report which caught the public mood, for it roundly condemned the Tay Bridge as badly designed, badly built, and badly maintained. Sir Thomas was held principally to blame. The Esk Viaduct was more like a seaside pier by comparison with the Tay Bridge, but Bouch had taken to heart the criticisms of the inadequate bolts in the ties at Dundee and he had the 1½in bolts connecting the diagonal bracing of the columns of the piers at Montrose replaced by 1¾in bolts, with the holes in the ties and lugs drilled out to give a snug fit. The diagonal ties too were increased in strength.

As the furore over the Tay Bridge slowly died away the North British set about the completion of the line into Montrose. With Bouch disgraced and dismissed, they sought the advice of W.R. Galbraith, then civil engineer to the London & South Western Railway, but a Scot by birth. On 21 October 1880, the N.B. Board received unsatisfactory reports on the South Esk Viaduct. Nine days later Bouch was dead, and W.R. Galbraith was invited to examine the South Esk Viaduct and give an opinion on what was needed to make the structure fit for approval by the Board of Trade. By 4 November Galbraith had submitted his findings, and was instructed to carry out any essential work forthwith. At the end of November Colonel Yolland, Chief Inspector of Railways, was on his way to Montrose, for there was no delegating the responsibility to examine a Bouch iron bridge in view of continued public misgivings. What he found on his arrival was even worse than he had feared.

A description of the viaduct was given in his report. It carried a single line and consisted of thirty pairs of lattice girders of 47ft span, braced together, and supported on 15in-diameter cast-iron columns, filled with concrete. These had been machined and drilled on the special machine at Middlesbrough, which had been built twenty years earlier for the Belah and Deepdale viaducts, and had been used subsequently on the Tay Bridge. The girders were 6ft deep, and supported at 9ft centres by the columns, which were cast in 12ft sections, and braced together by tiebars bolted to lugs cast in the columns. Although more robust and of a far lesser height, they possessed all the characteristics that had led to the fall of the Tay Bridge. The most remarkable feature was the provision of raking columns at every pier, but this was part of the original design, and not added as an afterthought following the Tay Bridge collapse.

The design of the girders was the work of Allan D. Stewart. He was an able designer, and his girders for the Tay Bridge were highly praised. Most of those were eventually transferred to the new bridge, and are still giving good service today. To complete the deck at Montrose, heavy timbers 14ft long were laid across the girders, and the longitudinal timber decking attached. Finally the permanent way was laid, and a single handrail of 2½in gas pipe in light cast-iron brackets was provided each side of the deck. As was Bouch's practice, the girders had been riveted end to end after erection, in groups of seven or eight. In theory this added considerable strength, but should any pier sink the extra stresses imposed on the girders could lead to failure when a train passed over. There was every chance that sinking would occur in the future.

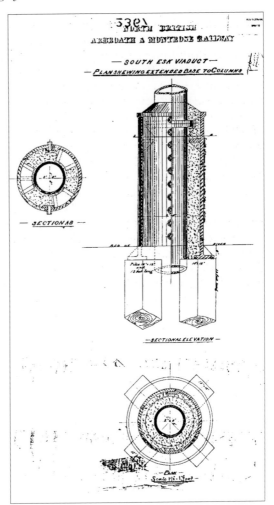

This is Bouch's drawing showing a modification to the piers on the South Esk Viaduct at Montrose. Built originally with the tubular cast-iron columns resting o the timber piles, movement under load was prevented by cast-iron jackets filled with concrete. Twelve foot piles in soft ground affected by strong tidal scour seem to be somewhat inadequate.

Yolland found the piers and the piling still showing the same faults which Raff had reported a year and a half before, and when a test load was placed on one of the piers it sank 2½ins. Other piers, except those on screw piles, showed a similar tendency. The check rails on the track were so placed that Yolland expressed his opinion that a derailment was 'not a very remote contingency'. He submitted recommendations which effectively meant complete rebuilding of the bridge, and declared it unfit for passenger traffic, though he had no power to prohibit the passage of goods trains at the Company's risk. Desperate though they were to commence traffic, this was a risk they wisely declined to take.

When the NBR Board next met in early January 1881, Galbraith, who meanwhile had been appointed in Bouch's place as consulting engineer, was instructed to carry out any work needed to make the viaduct passable for goods traffic. A decision was reached to commence running goods trains on 1 February. To cover themselves the North British wrote to Yolland, seeking his advice as to what safety precautions should be taken. Yolland replied at the beginning of February. He advised that no train should cross the bridge in less than 5 minutes 28 seconds. A man, designated as a 'speed regulator', should walk in front of every train at 3mph, and he should record the times of entering and leaving the viaduct. Any 'excesses' were to be reported. Shortly afterwards the crossing time was reduced to 4½ minutes, which meant a brisk walk for the unhappy 'regulator' pursued by an impatient driver.

The brick viaduct over a former branch of the South Esk at Montrose. This land has now been reclaimed.

The Lunan Viaduct on the Arbroarth to Montrose line. This had to be rebuilt as it was found on delivery that the rivets were too far apart, weakening the structure considerably.

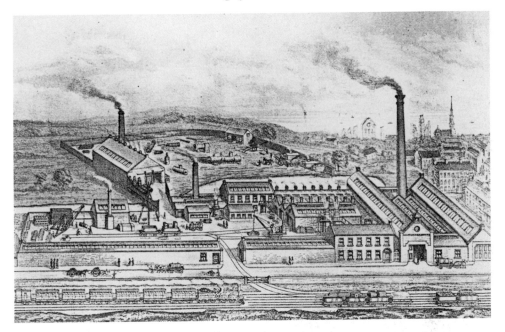

The Dens Iron Works on the northern outskirts of Arbroath, serving the fishing, farming and textile industries. Typical of the period, they could turn their hand to anything, and built five locomotives. The Arbroath & Montrose line is in the foreground.

A recent view of Ashorne House in Warwickshire. This was purchased by William Bouch, only son of Sir Thomas Bouch, in the early 1880s, and passed to Bouch's grandson, Thomas. He died in about 1950 and left no heirs

SIR THOMAS BOUCH
CIVIL ENGINEER
BORN 25 FEB. 1822
DIED 30 OCT. 1880

The headstone of Sir Thomas Bouch's grave in the Dean Cemetery, Edinburgh. This shows him around the time of his death in 1880 and is one of only three known portraits.

The North British Directors reluctantly bit the bullet, and asked Galbraith to design a new viaduct. He came up with a proposal for a bridge of sixteen spans, mostly of 96ft. The piers were to be of cast iron, 5ft in diameter above high water level, and 7½ft below. Galbraith chose a rather old-fashioned design of girder, with closely spaced lattice bracing, which was probably calculated to reassure travellers. The track ran between the girders, as suggested by Colonel Yolland. Tenders were in by the end of May 1881, and the successful contractor was William Arrol, with a tender of £23,855 5s 2d. Yolland inspected the new viaduct on 3 March 1883, and passenger trains started to cross on the first day of May.

Bouch's ramshackle structure was dismantled, and no trace remains. It is likely that the girders were reused elsewhere, for Arrol was not a man to waste good material, but there is no record of where they went. It would have been a final crushing blow to a stricken man had Bouch not died before his last bridge was completed, and as quickly condemned and dismantled.

It must be said, in fairness to Sir Thomas Bouch, that there were extenuating circumstances, for in 1879 and the first half of 1880 he was working under great stress. For several years he had been suffering from a chronic heart condition, and had been under continual pressure during the building of the Tay Bridge. Work on finalising the details of his Forth Bridge was piling up, and William Arrol, the contractor, was pressing for drawings to allow work to start. The destruction of the Tay Bridge, and the Inquiry which followed, occupied most of his time and energy for the first six months of 1880.

The Death of Sir Thomas Bouch

Mercifully, Bouch did not live to see the sad end of his viaduct at Montrose. The task of rebuilding was given to W.R. Galbraith, and the contractor was once again that most enterprising and reliable of men, William Arrol. In 1881 there remained a popular prejudice against iron bridges, and Galbraith chose a somewhat old-fashioned form of close lattice for the girders with the line passing between the girders rather than on top. This, he hoped, would provide an increased feeling of security to nervous travellers. Hopefully it still does.

On the surface Bouch showed no outward signs of his inner turmoil, and attended his office as usual. His increasing deafness was a great inconvenience to him, and his chronic heart problems were becoming worse. To his staff and those who met him he was no longer the man he had been, and was visibly failing. On 31 July he went down to London to progress the Edinburgh South Suburban Bill through Parliament and stayed there for a week. With the preamble of the Bill proved he returned to Edinburgh, where in the day following he was reported to be in a state of prostration. The next day he was still very unwell, and remained confined to the house for the following two months. His doctor advised him to go to the little spa town of Moffat in Dumfriesshire where he could find peace to recuperate. Before he could benefit from this advice he caught a chill, which he was too weak to fight, even had his spirit been willing, and pneumonia must have developed for he imperceptibly slipped away despite all Margaret's loving care. By 30 October he was dead, 'of a broken heart' as the *Illustrated London News* reported, quoting from *The Builder*, where it was sympathetically recorded. *The Builder's* obituary was in the flowery prose much favoured at the time. To quote a part:

> Any one who saw the late Sir Thomas Bouch moving to and fro during the Inquiry with which his name must for ever be associated, could not help seeing that he was a stricken man… The circumstances, in the mere aspect of their human interest and as a commentary on the vanity of human affairs, appear to us to afford the materials for a tragedy, the motive of which is peculiar to the times we live in. In the climax, when the fates have come with the shears, the end, instead of being the culmination of the sorrow, is rather of the nature of a kindly remedy for evils that could no longer be borne.

Some of the more heartless of the NBR shareholders showed little mercy, and even after his death his widow was hounded to pay compensation for her husband's errors of judgment. These human vultures wished to submit a claim against his estate, though their lawyers warned them that they had a poor case. The many obituary notices published were in generally neutral or broadly sympathetic terms, but what was, perhaps, surprising was that *The Engineer*, which had been generally supportive of Bouch in his lifetime, should turn so savagely against him when dead. After a general introduction listing Bouch's many achievements the writer continued:

> Some years ago the North British Railway Company spent £41,000 on what is now characterised [as] a preposterous project for crossing the Forth at Charleston, and it is a little surprising that after this ill-advised and ill-conceived piece of business he ever got much bridge work entrusted to him. [This refers to the 1864 Forth Bridge project at Blackness Point.]

In fact, it was the financial machinations of Richard Hodgson, who had succeeded John Learmonth as Chairman of the NBR, which nearly brought the Company to its knees, and forced the abandonment of Bouch's first Forth Bridge at an early stage. Hodgson was enormously powerful, enormously effective and utterly ruthless. When he was found to have been fiddling the books and paying dividends out of capital his end came swiftly. George Hudson and Richard Hodgson had much in common in their business ethics. It must of course be remembered too that down in London Bouch had always been regarded as an interloper, a mere provincial, and 'not one of us', even though for a while he had maintained an office in Westminster, managed by his chief assistant Mr Peddie. Now the 'Westminster Mafia' was taking its revenge.

The *Carlisle Journal* wrote of Bouch as a 'Cumberland worthy' and, after some introductory remarks, lifted a whole column of small print word for word from the obituary in *The Scotsman*.

Although in life Bouch had never sought public acclaim, and even failed to attend the occasion at Dundee when he was due to be presented with the Freedom of the City – it was rumoured that he was down in England consulting the steelmakers on the chains for his Forth Bridge – he had found his friends among the engineers, architects and business men of Edinburgh rather than the surgeons, doctors and lawyers in their New Town fastness. He had been a keen Member of Council at the Royal Scottish Society of Arts rather than seeking the higher realms of the Royal Society of Edinburgh. Even though in politics he was a staunch Liberal throughout his life he had never intruded his views on others.

He might have been surprised, and perhaps even a little gratified, at the turnout for his funeral at Holy Trinity Church at Dean Bridge, though even grander funerals were the order of the day. There was the customary panoply, the glass hearse, the four black horses with their nodding plumes, accompanied by black-clad mutes walking either side of the hearse. The Revd G.V. Faithful conducted the burial service, and the eight pallbearers carried the polished oak coffin to the hearse, which conveyed it to the Dean Cemetery for interment. The impressive cortege contained twenty mourning coaches and several private carriages, together with many mourners on foot.

Among the pall-bearers were his son William Bouch; Mr Hussey, his son-in-law from London; Mr Thomas Nelson, the railway contractor from Glasgow and father of Lady Bouch; Bouch's old schoolmaster, Joseph Hannah from Carlisle; and Mr Trimble CE, who was for many years Bouch's right-hand man. A strong contingent of Directors and officers from the North British Railway was present, and about thirty other mourners including Willam Arrol, Thomas Peddie, Charles Raff, and Charles Meik from Bouch's staff. Despite all Bouch's contribution to the profession over forty years there was nobody representing the Board of Trade or the Institution of Civil Engineers. A fine stone memorial carrying a bas-relief portrait can still be found among the weeds in the Dean Cemetery in Edinburgh.

It may fairly be said that Sir Thomas Bouch was as much a victim of the Tay Bridge as the seventy-five or so passengers and train crew who perished that night. The precise number is unknown and the Tay will for ever hold its secrets.

The Tay Bridge was rebuilt with William Henry Barlow as consulting engineer, and his son, Crawford Barlow, as resident engineer, and a very fine job they made of it. In 1890 John Fowler and Benjamin Baker, with the able assistance of Alan Duncan Stewart, had conquered the Forth at Queensferry where Bouch had planned his bridge. All that now remains of Bouch's stillborn venture is a small brick block on Inchgarvie Island bearing a navigation light.

According to John Prebble, Lady Bouch took the death of her husband very hard, and consoled herself with the bottle until later marrying a sea-captain. Be that as it may, William gave up engineering, a demanding profession probably never to his taste, and used his inheritance to buy a small country estate at Ashorne in Warwickshire, where he lived the life of a country gentleman. A son, Thomas, was born at Ashorne, and died there in the middle of the last century. Sir Thomas became regarded as the black sheep of the family, and, according to a distant relative, was not to be spoken of in front of the children and servants. Fortunately, the only known photograph of Bouch, showing him in his prime, was loaned to John Prebble and published in the first edition of *The High Girders* and reproduced on page 8.

The Last Will and Testament of Sir Thomas Bouch

Will dated 16 August 1878
Deposited at General Register House 17 November 1880

Note: This is not taken from the original but from the legally certified copy deposited at General Register House.

It is a very long and complicated will in relation to the number of legacies and bequests, though the estate was a very valuable one, worth many millions today. Provision was made for all likely eventualities and some unlikely ones. In all it ran to forty-nine pages of clerky copperplate, easy to decipher. The Inventory, which lists all Sir Thomas's financial affairs, is, by comparison, slapdash and more difficult to make sense of after all these years. The details below are extremely brief extracts and only a layman's interpretation of the legal niceties. There are extraordinarily few bequests outside the family circle, and Bouch may have advised his Trustees informally of his wishes. Even his unmarried sister at Thursby did not receive a legacy, except an annuity of £50 pa, but she had established her position and may not have needed the money. Not a single worthy cause is named, which is unusual.

When Thomas Bouch went to Scotland in 1849, he seems to have cut himself off from all but close family. It may have been his uncle, Martin, who founded the Liverpool branch of the family. It is believed that he also had an aunt.

The following persons were nominated as Trustees:

Ann Bouch (sister) of Thursby near Carlisle. Spinster.
John Walker, General Manager of the North British Railway.
Andrew John Dickson, Family Solicitor.
William Bouch (son), after reaching the age of twenty-five.

Conditions:

1. The Trustees to pay all debts, funeral charges etc.

2. MARGARET TERRIE BOUCH (wife) to receive:
   a) All horses, carriages and contents of stables.
   b) Wines, liquors and consumables, stores and provisions.
   c) The sum of £1,500 to cover urgent disbursements.

3. To WILLIAM BOUCH (son) the sum of £15,000.
   To WILLIAM BOUCH, the whole of the Professional and Scientific books in the library.

4. To FANNY BOUCH and ELIZABETH ANN BOUCH (daughters) the sum of £10,000 each.

5. To senior office staff GEORGE TRIMBLE, JAMES PEDDIE and R.O. RODDICK £500 each.

6. To his Wife for her lifetime, providing that she does not remarry, all income from his estate, together with all household goods, chattels and statuary etc.

Note: As he prospered, Bouch seems to have started collecting statuary from abroad, according to correspondence among his office papers now in the Scottish National Archives.

7. To ELIZABETH ANN (sister and spinster) an annuity of £50 pa.

8. The residue of his estate to go to WILLIAM BOUCH (son) on attaining the age of twenty-five.

9. To JOHN WALKER if he accepts the duties of a Trustee, the sum of £250.

The Inventory of Sir Thomas Bouch:

This does not contain a list of goods and chattels as might be supposed, but lists all debts and investments, or any other money due to the Estate such as loans and mortgages. There is a loan of £500 made to his father-in-law, THOMAS NELSON, of Glasgow.

APPENDICES

I

The Railways of Sir Thomas Bouch

Name	Act	Opened
Arbroath & Montrose Railway	--/--/--	01/03/81
Blairgowrie branch	--/--/--	01/08/55
Cockermouth, Keswick & Pemrith	01/08/61	02/01/65
Crieff & Methven Railway	--/--/--	21/05/66
Crieff Junction & Crieff	15/08/53	14/03/56
Darlington & Barnard Castle	03/07/54	08/07/56
Devon Valley Railway (part)	23/07/58	01/05/63
Eden Valley. Kirkby Stephen	21/05/58	08/04/62
Edinburgh, Loanhead & Roslin	20/06/70	02/07/77
Edinburgh Suburban & South Side Junction	26/08/80	01/12/84
Esk Valley (Polton branch)	21/07/63	15/04/67
Fife & Kinross Railway	--/07/55	20/08/58
Glasgow & Coatbridge	--/--/--	01/02/71

Kinross-shire Railway	--/--/57	20/01/60
Kirriemuir branch	--/--/--	15/11/54
Lancashire Union Railway	13/07/57	08/08/61
Leadburn, Linton & Dolphinton	03/06/62	04/07/64
Leuchars to Wormit (Tay Bridge)	--/--/70	30/05/78
Leven Railway	--/--/--	10/08/54
Leslie Railway	07/07/57	01/02/61
Newport (Wormit and Tayport)	--/--/--	13/05/79
Peebles Railway	08/07/53	04/07/55
Penicuik Railway	20/06/70	02/09/72
Swanley, Sevenoaks & Maidstone (Bat and Ball)	--/--/59	02/06/62
Maidstone East	--/--/72	01/06/74
St Andrews Railway	03/07/51	01/07/52
South Durham & Lancashire Union	13/07/57	08/08/61
Waverley to Granton cutoff	--/--/--	22/03/68

II

Bouch and His Bridge in Literature

Thomas Bouch was by nature a private man who did not seek the limelight, although there were occasions when it could not be escaped. His greatest achievements were the Stainmore line, with its two towering viaducts at Belah and Deepdale, and the Tay Bridge, ill-fated though it proved to be.

Poets of all kinds, from the sublime to the ridiculous, were accorded more popular respect then than now, and could always find a corner in some local newspaper. There were some who became widely known in their localities, and who managed to scrape a living by selling their products in broadsheets at country markets. Among these was Poet Close who dwelt at Poet's Hall, Kirkbuy Stephen in Westmorland. The author of books like Kirkby-Stephen Cricket Papers, 'Bring Flowers', the wondrous story of a poet's life, Priestcraft and Purgatory, and a Comic Drama in 3 Acts called 'The Wise Men of Gotham' who, it will be remembered, went to sea in a bowl.

In September 1859 he published a poem of twenty-nine quatrains, entitled Beelah [sic] Viaduct on Stainmore, Westmoreland [sic], the 'Wonder of the Age', and dedicated it to Thomas Bouch Esq. CE. An illustration at the head showed the poet declaiming his work to Bouch – one suspects poetic licence here. A short extract will give the flavour:

Oh Bouch! What a prolific Brain is thine,
To scheme at first this strange gigantic plan;
Thine Eye could scan our rugged Hills and Vales
Such genius proves thee a superior man.
He said 'It can, it MUST be done!' and lo!
From Middlesbro' came forth the clever men
Who'd catched a spark of Bouch's electric fire
And flashing Thought began its work again.

But when 'The Archangel's Trump shall sound'
As good John Wesley piously he sings;
May we among the heav'nly host be found
When we have bid farewell to earthly things.

The great curving viaduct at Deepdale, although not quite on the scale of Belah, was ignored by the rhymers.

When the Belah Viaduct was being demolished, the following verse was found among papers deposited under the central pier on 6 September 1859:

To future ages these lines will tell
Who built this structure o'er the dell.
Gilkes Wilson with their eighty men
Raised Belah's Viaduct oe'r the glen.

Another poet, Charles Davis Brough, penned the following:

See! Now Beelah's [sic] beautious sights begin!
Whose curling stream shall ever flow within,
And underneath this splendid monster bridge,
Shall floods henceforth descend from every ridge;
Westmorelnd's [sic] honour form'd by the skill of man
Shall ever o'er thy spacious landscape span,
And thousands wonder at the glorious sight,
When trains will run aloft both day and night,
For ages past, no human tongue could tell
Of such a structure o'er thy monster gill
Time will roll on, and mortals may increase
When those who see it now, we hope will rest in Peace.

The Tay Bridge was far more in the public eye and aroused strong passions when first proposed. John Prebble tells of Patrick Matthew, the Seer of Gourdiehill in the Carse of Gowrie. He was a simple man, claiming the power of second sight, and he did not like the idea of the bridge at all. At every opportunity he spoke and wrote and generally fulminated against it. Unlike most of the other opponents he had no axe to grind and his personal views were respected by the local people though he was the butt of the Press. He prophesied doom and destruction for the bridge should it ever be built. Said he: 'the tremendous impetus of the icy blast must wrench off the girders as if they were a spider's web, or hurl the whole construction before it'. Even as the bridge proposals were going ahead with the opposition placated or bought off, Patrick Matthew voiced his fears once again: 'the foundation of the piers will, we may expect, be very unequal, very unsafe, or very costly; some of them standing as firm as the rock itself, others as false as the foundation of the Royal Exchange'. He went on: 'in the case of accident with a heavy passenger train on the bridge the whole of the passengers will be killed. The eels will come to gloat over in delight the horrible wreck and banquet'. He was dead within the year, but the eels would eventually dine well on the number of bodies which were never recovered.

By contrast, William McGonagall of Dundee admired the bridge as he watched it rise. Often described as the world's worst poet, a charge that is quite unjustifiable, he was as much entitled to be respected as a primitive poet as are primitive artists. Certainly he did not lack a sense of humour served up with a straight face when he told of 'The Famous Tay Whale'. These verses on the Tay Bridge are those most often quoted:

> Beautiful Bridge of the Silvery Tay!
> And prosperity to Messrs Bouche [sic] and Grothe,
> The famous engineers of the present day,
> Who have succeeded in erecting the Railway
> Bridge of the Silvery Tay,
> Which stands unequalled to be seen
> Near by Dundee and the Magdalen Green.

By 1880 he had to write of the disaster. His last verse reads:

> It must have been an awful sight,
> To witness in the dusky moonlight,
> While the Storm Fiend did laugh and angry did bray,
> Along the Railway Bridge of the Silv'ry Tay.
> Oh! Ill fated Bridge of the Silv'ry Tay,
> I must now conclude my lay
> By telling the world fearlessly without the least dismay,
> That your central girders would not have given way,
> At least many sensible men do say,
> Had they been supported on each side with buttresses,
> At least many a sensible man confesses,
> For the stronger we our houses do build,
> The less chance we have of being killed.

The itinerant street ballad-mongers of Dundee hawked their wares to the crowds awaiting news of those lost in the accident, and these may have reached the ears of Bouch in the Royal Hotel. John Prebble quoted one verse:

> There a crash – an instant's glaring,
> Unheard shrieks and prayers ablending,
> Hearts a breaking, iron rending,
> One dark plunge – the work is done!

While the fall of the Tay Bridge was a national disaster it also had worldwide repercussions especially on the Continent, where there was some ill-concealed satisfaction that the self-satisfied if not arrogant British engineers had received their comeuppance. For the previous thirty years, since the visit of Karl Culmann of the Bavarian State Railways, there had been envy that the ill-educated British engineers had access to so much capital compared with their Continental colleagues. But all that was to change. The fall of the Ashtabula Creek Bridge in America two years earlier, when, due to a broken casting, a whole train was plunged into an icy river with great loss of life, had concentrated the minds of American bridge engineers as never before, and the British would in time follow, though their minds were concerned with wind forces.

During the latter half of the nineteenth century the German-speaking states had overtaken the French in the development of structural theory, and it was in Germany that the fall of the Tay Bridge produced a particularly strong impression. A young German writer, Max von Eyth, produced a semi-fictional account, based on the facts but changing many of the names. Von Eyth was himself a trained engineer and could understand the complexities of the story. His volume of stories and light verse was published in 1899 under the title *Hinter Pflug und Schraubstock*, and it was the last story 'Beraufstragik' which told the tale of the Tay Bridge.

The story concerning the bridge is generally factually correct. Names and personalities are generally changed and the origins can only be guessed from the context. Bouch becomes 'William Bruce' and Henry Noble alone is given his own name. There is romantic interest where Von Eyth marries Bruce's daughter. The end of the bridge is told only briefly:

> The gale grew ever fiercer as the train of six carriages disappeared into the pitch blackness, carrying with it seventy-five passengers and crew. The rear lights were soon out of sight, but watchers on the north bank later spoke of having seen sparks, presumably from the engine wheels grinding on the check-rails. Then several flashes of flame.

The German poet, Theodor Fontane, was quick off the mark, for on 10 January 1880 he published his poem entitled 'The Tay Bridge'. The late Professor Jack Simmons included an English translation in his book, *Railways: An Anthology*. It may have lost something in the translation and its approach is mainly philosophical. To quote one verse only:

> On the north side, the bridgemaster's house –
> All its windows look to the south,
> And the bridgemaster's men, restless and agitated,
> Anxiously keep watch to the south;
> For the wind began to sport more violently,
> And then, it was as though fire fell from the heavens,
> And plummeted in glowing splendour
> Above the waters below … and then again all was darkness.

In May 1931 the popular author, Dr A.J. Cronin, first published his book *Hatter's Castle*. This proved enormously popular and by 1940 had reached its twenty-seventh impression despite wartime paper rationing. Cronin was probably the first British author to incorporate the saga of the Tay Bridge in the body of his narrative. Even in 1931, half a century on, Cronin was taking a chance in stirring up old memories, for there would still be many alive in Dundee who remembered that fateful night. He tells of a young Irishman, Denis Foyle, who takes that last train from Edinburgh to attend a job interview in Dundee on the Monday and with his wedding planned for the next day. Cronin describes those last few anguished seconds as the bridge buckled and fell:

> Then, abruptly, when the train lay enwrapped within the iron lamellae of the middle link of the bridge, the wind elevated itself with a culminating, exultant roar to the orgasm of its power and passion: the bridge broke. Steel girders snapped like twigs, cement crumbled like sand, iron pillars bent like willow wands. The middle span melted like wax. Its wreckage clung around the tortured train, which gyrated madly for an instant in space. Immediately, a shattering rush of broken glass and wood descended upon Denis, cutting and bruising him with mangling violence. He felt the wrenching torsion of metal, and the grating of falling masonry.

Cronin's knowledge of metallurgy was rather primitive. There was no steel in the first Tay Bridge and very little in the second. Cast-iron pillars would shatter rather than bend.

In 1976 Alanna Knight, an Edinburgh author, built her novel, *A Drink for the Bridge*, around the Tay Bridge disaster nearly a century earlier. Her description is as dramatic as Cronin's:

> Now the wind pounced roaring upon the train, like a savage animal devouring its helpless prey. The train see-sawed, trembling, the roaring around it deafening. There was a grinding tearing

noise that seemed to shatter Pete's head. And other screams now, the blonde woman's louder than any though, as outside the compartment something wrenched away. The noise was ear-splitting. He struggled to his feet, but the floor slipped away from him again as outside the last iron thread, holding together the great iron girders, snapped. He was thrown round, down and round again and the world turned black and fell into eternity.

SELECT BIBLIOGRAPHY

Books and References to the Tay Bridge and other works of Sir Thomas Bouch, 1822–1880.

Berridge, P.S.A., *The Girder Bridge* (Robert Maxwell, Pergamon, London, 1969). Pp 12-30

Board of Trade, The Tay Bridge Inquiry (HMSO, 1880. The official report of the Commissioners. Public Record Office. PARL Papers, 1880. [c2616] XXXIX)

Bowtell, Harold, *Rails Through Lakeland* (Silver Link, 1989)

Brodie, R., The Reminiscences of a Civil Engineering Contractor. (Wright, 1943). Pp 6-9. Report of a hurricane at Cupar, 28 December 1879

Byrom, Bernard, *Railways of Upper Strathearn* (Oakwood Press, 2004)

Casualty List: Official casualty list published by Dundee Police, 1880. Sixty-four bodies found or missing.

Cronin, A.J., *Hatter's Castle* (Gollancz, London, first printed 1931)

Dow, William M., 'Destined for Disaster' (*The Scots Magazine*, December 1989). Pp 275-286

Earnshaw, Alan, Sir Thomas Bouch: Hero or Villain? (Backtrack Atlantic Transport Publishers, Penryn, Sept/Oct 1991). Vol. 5, No. 5, pp 233-240

Fontane, Theodore, 'The Tay Bridge' poem published in Jack Simmons (Ed.), *Railways, An Anthology*, (Collins, London, 1991). Pp 81-3

Gilkes, Edgar, 'The Tay Bridge'. Paper and discussion. (The Cleveland Institution of Engineers, 1866-7). Pp 12-37

Groethe, Albert, *The Tay Bridge* (Dundee, April, 1878). P.89

Harman, F.W., *The Gilkes, Wilson and Hopkins Partnerships* (Century Locoprints, Toddington (nd)).

Hoole, K., *The Stainmore Railway* (Dalesman Publishing, Clapham/Yorkshire, 1973)

Hoole, K., *The Stockton & Darlington Railway in Pictures* (David & Charles, Newton Abbot, 1975)

Hopkins, H.J., *A Span of Bridges* (David Charles, Newton Abbot, 1970). Pp 149-155

Hurst, Jeff, *The Glencorse Branch* (Oakwood press, 1999)

Hutchinson, C.S., Report to the Boasrd of Trade on Inspection of the Tay Bridge, 25-27 February 1878. (Public Record Office. Parl Papers, 1880). [c2624] LXIII 459

Knight, Alanna, *A Drink for the Bridge* (Macmillan, London, 1976)

Law, J.N.C., 'Sir Thomas Bouch – A Scapegoat?' *Railway Magazine*, March 1965. *Correspondence*, September 1965

Leng, John, *The Tay Bridge Guide* (Dundee, 1887)

Lewis, Peter R., *The Beautiful Railway Bridge of the Silvery Tay* (Tempus, Stroud, 2004)

MacGonagall, William, 'The Tay Bridge' poem published in *Selected Poems Part 2* (Berlin/Edinburgh, 1993). Pp 43-53

Marshall, Peter, *The Peebles Railway* (Oakwood Press, Usk, 2005)

Martin & Macleod, 'The Tay Bridge Disaster. A Study in Structural Pathology'. Proceedings of the Forth Bridge Centenary Conference. Spon. 1990, pp 405-414. See also Proc ICE Vol. 108, May 1995 pp 77-83 and Nov. 1996, pp 185-6

Mawson, Paquita, Vision of Steel. Chapter 2. The Tay Bridge. Biography of G.D. Delpratt, a Dutch engineering pupil working on the bridge. (Published in Australia)

Paxton, Roland (Ed.), 100 Years of the Forth Bridge. Thomas Telford. (1990)

Pottgeisser, Hans, *Eisenbahnbrucken aus zwei Jahrhunderten. Die Brucker uber den Firth of Tay in Schottland* (German text. Birhauser Verlag, Basel, 1985). Pp 209-216

Preeble, John, *The High Girders* (Secker & Warburg, London, 1956)

Shipway, J.S., *The Tay Bridge* (Institution of Civil Engineers, Edinburgh, 1987)

Spink, G.W., 'The Rise and Fall of the Tay Bridge' (*The Railway Magazine*, Jan/Feb/March 1970)

Swale, W.E. (Tr.), Novel evidence on the Tay Bridge disaster. A semi-fictional account by Max von Eyth. Published in German. (Stuttgart, 1899). Translation and comments in ICE Library

Swinfen, David, *The Fall of the Tay Bridge* (Mercat Press, Edinburgh, 1994)

Thomas, John, *The North British Railway Vol. I* (David & Charles, Newton Abbot, 1969). Pp 218-37

Thomas, John, *The Tay Bridge Disaster* (David & Charles, Newton Abbot, 1972)

Thomas, John, *Forgotten Railways: Scotland* (David & Charles, Newton Abbot, 1981)

Thomas, John, *Regional History Vol. 6: Scottish Lowlands* (David & Charles, Newton Abbot. Revised 1984 by Alan J. Paterson)

Thomas, John and Turnock, David *Regional History Vol. 15: Scottish Highlands* (David & Charles, Newton Abbot, 1989)

Walton, Peter, *The Stainmore and Eden Valley Lines* (Oxford Publishing, Sparkford, 1992)

INDEX

Page numbers in italics indicate an illustration.

Thursby

Portraits and Personalities

Rise and Fall of the Tay Bridge

The Tay Bridge Court of Inquiry, 1880